"Since the early church first began to present the gospel as an apologetic that corresponded to the philosophical categories of Greek thought, we have tried to reduce biblical truths to constructs. Our earliest creeds necessarily followed this approach. But such constructs do not always capture the heart or move us deeper into the journey of faith. Though this approach was not entirely wrong we missed a whole range of biblical meanings that corresponded more closely with the imagery actually employed by the biblical writers themselves. Neil Livingstone gives us a thrilling book that shows us practically how to expand the way we present the gospel, first to ourselves and then to outsiders. This is an inspiring and fruitful book that will foster a needed rethinking of how we share Christ. I heartily commend it."

JOHN H. ARMSTRONG, PRESIDENT, ACT 3, CAROL STREAM, ILLINOIS

"How can the lives of Christ's followers become gospel tapestries? Neil Livingstone weaves the life-struggles of contemporary Americans together with biblical images of salvation in order to exemplify what it means to incarnate the good news. Readers will be challenged not only to know about the life-transforming power of the gospel but genuinely to embody it."

JOEL B. GREEN, PROFESSOR OF NEW TESTAMENT INTERPRETATION, ASBURY THEOLOGICAL SEMINARY, AND AUTHOR OF RECOVERING THE SCANDAL OF THE CROSS

"The gospel is never less; it's always more. By expanding the metaphors and rationalities with which we understand and explain the gospel, Neil Livingstone does the church (and the world) a great service. Without disparaging propositional truth, he adds a layer of aesthetic truth, and in so doing, exhibits the beauty of the good news."

TONY JONES, NATIONAL COORDINATOR OF EMERGENT VILLAGE (WWW.EMERGENTVILLAGE.COM), AND AUTHOR OF THE SACRED WAY: SPIRITUAL PRACTICES FOR EVERYDAY LIFE

"Too often we limit the gospel to one aspect of life. Neil Livingstone walks us through a number of the Bible's powerful portraits of God's work in a way that enriches our life and witness."

TREMPER LONGMAN III, ROBERT H. GUNDRY PROFESSOR OF BIBLICAL STUDIES, WESTMONT COLLEGE, AND AUTHOR OF READING THE BIBLE WITH HEART AND MIND

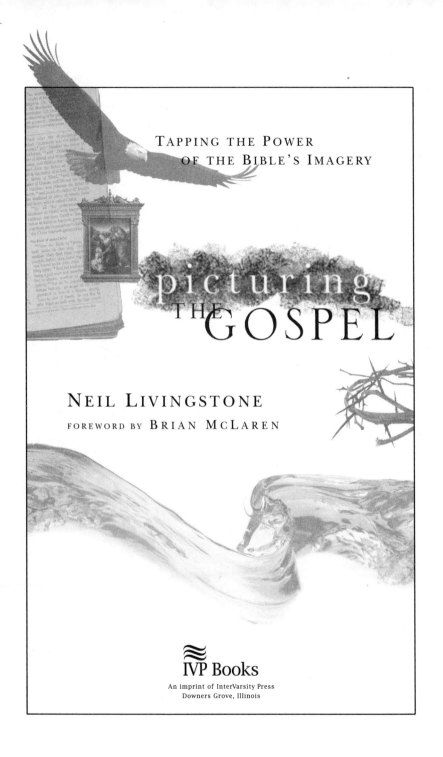

TAPPING THE POWER
OF THE BIBLE'S IMAGERY

picturing
THE
GOSPEL

NEIL LIVINGSTONE

FOREWORD BY BRIAN MCLAREN

IVP Books

An imprint of InterVarsity Press
Downers Grove, Illinois

InterVarsity Press
P.O. Box 1400, Downers Grove, IL 60515-1426
World Wide Web: www.ivpress.com
E-mail: email@ivpress.com

InterVarsity Press® is the book-publishing division of InterVarsity Christian Fellowship/USA®, a student movement active on campus at hundreds of universities, colleges and schools of nursing in the United States of America, and a member movement of the International Fellowship of Evangelical Students. For information about local and regional activities, write Public Relations Dept., InterVarsity Christian Fellowship/USA, 6400 Schroeder Rd., P.O. Box 7895, Madison, WI 53707-7895, or visit the IVCF website at <www.intervarsity.org>.

While all the stories in this book are true, some names and identifying details have been changed to protect the privacy of those involved.

Design: Cindy Kiple

Images: holy family: Erich Lessing / Art Resource, NY
water: Shinichi Maruyama/Getty Images
Bible: Mike Bentley/Getty Images
thorns: Jill Fromer/istockphoto.com
eagle: Sebastian Breham/istockphoto.com

ISBN 978-0-8308-3370-2

Printed in the United States of America ∞

Library of Congress Cataloging-in-Publication Data
Livingstone, Neil, 1962-
Picturing the Gospel: tapping the power of the Bible's imagery/
Neil Livingstone
 p. cm
Includes bibliographical references.
ISBN-13 978-0-8308-3370-2 (pbk.: alk. paper)
ISBN-10 978-0-8308-3370-6 (pbk.: alk. paper)
1. Bible. N.T.—Criticism, interpretation, etc. 2. Jesus
Christ—Person and offices. I. Title.
BS2361.3.L58 2007
225.6'4—dc22

                                                                2006038975

| **P** | 19 | 18 | 17 | 16 | 15 | 14 | 13 | 12 | 11 | 10 | 9 | 8 | 7 | 6 | 5 | 4 | 3 | 2 | 1 |
| **Y** | 23 | 22 | 21 | 20 | 19 | 18 | 17 | 16 | 15 | 14 | 13 | 12 | 11 | 10 | 09 | 08 | 07 | | | |

CONTENTS

FOREWORD

Philosophers often use the word *reductionistic* to describe the modern Western world. In doing so, they're describing a habit that, like many habits, can be helpful but, if taken to excess, can become problematic.

Reductionism is the habit of "boiling things down" or "putting things in a nutshell." For example, the statement "The universe is a clock, and God is the intelligent designer of the clock" makes certain things clear and accessible, but it can obscure and distort other things.

We Christians haven't been immune to this habit. The Bible, for example, gives us "the gospel" in four Gospel accounts, plus a number of letters and other supporting documents, but we often want to boil down the gospel to Romans 3:23 or put it in the nutshell of John 3:16. We want to reduce it to a formula that can be conveyed in a short booklet or diagrammed on a restaurant placemat.

Again, doing so can be helpful. I've filled up a lot of placemats myself in a lot of restaurants in my attempts to share the gospel with a friend. But we need to be on the alert for the ways we can take boiling, nutshelling and otherwise reducing to excess.

That's why the book you've just begun reading is so important and valuable. Neil Livingstone loves the gospel, and he loves the Bible, and he wants to help you counter reductionism by giving you a guided tour of the rich gallery of metaphors available to communicate the good news of Jesus.

A less useful book would attack one kind of reductionism and replace it with a competing one. But this book is like a photo album. It will show you a wide variety of photos that capture different sides of the "personality" of the gospel. When you're finished, you'll feel you know the gospel in a deeper way. You'll see how rich and deep and multifaceted it is. And in the process you'll learn how to think more creatively and theologically—not an insignificant byproduct!

If you take advantage of the various exercises at the end of the book and—even better—if you invite a group of friends to read the book and do the exercises together, I am confident that something wonderful will happen. Of course, you'll get a better picture of the good news, which is wonderful enough. But beyond that, through extended, prayerful and shared reflection on the gospel in its amazing richness and depth, you will experience transformation by it.

This is the tragedy of a boiled down or reduced gospel: it has only a fraction of the transforming power of the robust, rich, multilayered and multi-textured gospel. I guess little nutshells were made to be broken open so that from their seed a huge tree can grow.

I've known Neil for many years, and I've seen his passion for the gospel consistently call him forward in his journey as a disciple and a leader. He lives what he teaches, and he is a truly good teacher. Of course, you're about to find that out for yourself.

Brian McLaren
Author/activist (brianmclaren.net)

ENTER THE GALLERY

One night last year, I walked into a meeting late and no one noticed. It was a Christian gathering well underway at a local university. I strolled right in, and not a head turned in my direction. It wasn't because the students weren't friendly; they're usually quite welcoming. It wasn't because folks didn't know me; quite a few did. It wasn't that there was a lot of noise at the moment; in fact it was quite still. All eyes were on a young woman up front. She had no training as a speaker, yet she held every ounce of their attention. She was doing this by simply telling them her story.

Outwardly a together person with a strong faith, she had been secretly struggling with anorexia. And she'd been losing. But God had broken into her life with power and begun to heal her mind and heart. As she told of her struggle and of God's touch on her life, those of us listening leaned in and got even quieter. We knew we weren't hearing some vague religious words; this was real. This was Janine, our friend, and God had saved her.

So often, if the truth be told, the gospel message is just another sermon to be endured. But the story of Janine's good news got our attention. Where is that power when the gospel is usually spoken? The gospel should be that compelling every time it is heard. This is a book about finding that power, letting it touch our lives and energize our message.

What makes words like Janine's so riveting, so clear and powerful? When we hear these stories, we know we are hearing something real. We can tell that these people, who are just like us, have been touched by something big. And when they tell us their story, we feel we can almost touch it too.

These people end up speaking the gospel with clarity and power, not because of any training but because they are talking about what they themselves have experienced and come to understand. That's the way the gospel first broke into the world. Here's how the apostle John says it:

> That which was from the beginning, which we have heard, which we have seen with our eyes, which we have looked at and our hands have touched—this we proclaim concerning the Word of life. The life appeared; we have seen it and testify to it, and we proclaim to you the eternal life, which was with the Father and has appeared to us. We proclaim to you what we have seen and heard, so that you also may have fellowship with us. And our fellowship is with the Father and with his Son, Jesus Christ. (1 John 1:1-3)

We proclaim what we have seen, heard and touched. To speak the gospel with the clarity and power it deserves, we need to let it touch us. John (the apostle) and Janine (the student) were both touched by the power of the gospel, and they knew it. A deep reality had a hold on them, and they could name it: Jesus. Making that connection gave them a clear and powerful message to share. It sounds simple, but many Christians are missing that dynamic connection of life and gospel. And it is paralyzing our witness. But we need more than being touched by the gospel. We need to understand what has touched us.

MISSING THE CONNECTION

I think I can help you see this in a group of college students I knew. It was a fine Saturday morning at the George Washington University in D.C., and there they were, sitting in a classroom, waiting for me to teach them. What would draw busy college students to a seminar on a Saturday morning? Desperation. They needed help, and they knew it. They had a deep desire to proclaim what they "had seen and heard." They knew God was good and Jesus must be good news for their friends. But they felt their words were powerless. What they proclaimed often didn't seem to be real life, but some boring, irrelevant, religious verbiage.

They had been touched by "that which was from the beginning," and they would be able to proclaim him, but first there were some connections they needed to make. Two signs of the critical disconnection were clear in the first five minutes.

In those first few minutes, before I taught them anything, I wanted to see what they had already. I had them pair up and share the gospel as they knew it. I was paired with Jim. He obviously believed in God, but it was painful to watch him try to explain it. I felt like I was watching him rummage through a drawer of unorganized photos, occasionally drawing one out at random and commenting on it. He had the experiences with God, but he did not know how they spoke the good news.

Others in the room had been very well trained. They quickly and cleanly produced a standard gospel outline, complete with diagram. But there was little power there, for all the clarity. That outline didn't touch their lives and didn't promise much connection to many of their friends either. It was like a picture from someone else's album, an experience not theirs or from so long ago they had all but forgotten it. They had a picture to paint, but it wasn't rising up from within them.

Jim had stories of God's work, but he didn't know how to connect them to the gospel. The well-trained students had an outline, but they hadn't connected it to their own stories—and they knew it would not connect with the lives of their friends either.

These believers needed more than an outline or a personal story from years ago. What they needed was a way to understand how God had touched every part of their lives. They needed both to have the experiences with God and to be able to see how those experiences were connected to the good news of Jesus. They needed to have pictures of his work in their own life's album, and they needed to know how to open that up for others. They needed the life of the gospel and the words to picture it.

THE RESOURCES OF SCRIPTURE

The New Testament writers can help them, and many of us, make this connection of gospel and life. In this book we will be letting them teach us how the gospel touches every area of our lives. And if we listen, they will point the way to how we can speak a gospel that can also powerfully touch the lives of the people around us.

These first believers heard, saw and touched a Word of life that met them at every level of their lives. The one Lord had moved among them and touched them in many ways, giving them many gospel stories to tell, many sides of his glory to wonder at. They encountered him and came to understand what he meant in their lives, and so they had a powerful story to tell. And they found powerful ways to tell it.

COLORFUL LANGUAGE

The living Lord inspired living language, and lots of it. To understand and tell of Jesus, those early followers told stories, borrowed terms and picked up metaphors that helped them grasp what Jesus had done. They were not interested in abstract theories of religion, but in life. British evangelist and scholar John Stott says, "'Images' of salvation (or of the atonement) is a better term than 'theories.' For theories are usually abstract and speculative concepts, whereas biblical images of the atoning achievement of Christ are concrete pictures and belong to the data of revelation."[1] Our "data" from the Bible are vibrant images of Jesus and his work in our lives. The first disciples found a real-life Savior and told of him in concrete, real-life ways.

The first witnesses give us a variety of vivid and concrete pictures. Sometimes they tell us stories. In the Gospels they show us incidents in Jesus' life and things he said, stories carefully chosen to show his character and the nature of his work. Sometimes, in the letters, they work with extended metaphors. And sometimes they simply bring in terms that conjure up associations for us. For example, to say "Savior" to a Jewish audience would bring to mind the God who brought his people up from Egypt with "a mighty hand and an outstretched arm" (Deuteronomy 4:34). A Greek would imagine a semi-divine hero figure coming to the rescue. Both would have associations, mental pictures and feelings aroused by these words. These believers took up the common palettes of their cultures and used them to portray the new thing they had seen in Jesus.

Let's take a look at Ephesians, where Paul uses several images to talk of God's work in Christ:

> Praise be to the God and Father of our Lord Jesus Christ, who has blessed us in the heavenly realms with every spiritual blessing in Christ. For he chose us in him before the creation of the world to be holy and blameless in his sight. In love he predestined us to be adopted as his sons through Jesus Christ, in accordance with his pleasure and will—to the praise of his glorious grace, which he has freely given us in the One he loves. In him we have redemption through his blood, the forgiveness of sins, in accordance with the riches of God's grace that he lavished on us with all wisdom and understanding. (Ephesians 1:3-8)

Paul here is overwhelmed with the fullness and diversity of God's gifts in Jesus. It's not hard to imagine his eyes shining as he begins to speak of this amazing reality he has experienced. We have "every spiritual blessing in Christ." As he shows us just some of them, we see a quick parade of images and associations. The Father "predestined us to be adopted as his sons." We could attach a detailed, theological description to the adoption that happens in Jesus, but we are first called to consider a direct and wonderfully warm analogy with a concrete event in our natural world. A child is taken into a family "in love" because the parents have decided—and are glad—to do it. This is the central picture painted in this passage.

But it is not the only association called up here. We also have "redemption" through his blood. The same reality is being described, but from another angle. We are purchased or ransomed out of a bad situation, like Israel rescued from Egypt or a slave whose freedom is bought. But even the expansion needs to be expanded. The redemption is also a "forgiveness," another picture of blessing. *Forgiveness* is an accounting word. The Jews had used this picture for a long time to think of sin; sin meant you owed God, big. But he wanted to release you and cover over your debt.

This witness, Paul, seems compelled to use a rich variety of images when he speaks of Jesus. Only by using these together can he tell the story of the one event that touches our lives in so many ways, an event that gives us "innumerable benefits." In the Anglican Book of Common Prayer, the church is taught to pray "we remember his blessed passion and precious death, his mighty resurrection and glorious ascension; rendering unto thee most hearty thanks for the innumerable benefits procured unto us by the same."[2] It seems that the "riches of God's grace that he has lavished on us" are simply too big for one word or one image.

A GALLERY OF GOSPEL IMAGES

And Paul is just one writer, beginning one letter. The reality that had touched these pastors and evangelists was big, as big as the need of the whole world. Jesus had touched these people in many ways, so they had many sides of the good news they could tell.

The assortment of images that these writers used makes the Bible like a gallery. It is a place where we can wander and see many portrayals of God's saving work. Each image tells the gospel story: what Jesus did and how it affects our lives. Each one gives us a different angle, together giving us a complete picture of the work of God in Christ.

We have a many-sided gospel to know and proclaim. New Testament scholar Leon Morris calls it a "multifaceted salvation, one which may be regarded in many ways and which is infinitely satisfying."[3] Infinitely satisfying. The Bible's gallery of gospel images is going to be the key for us in this book, as we explore how to become more alive as witnesses. The many images of God's work will show us the many ways he can touch our lives. As we are touched in more ways by the gospel, we will see more ways it can touch the people around us. As we see the gospel more clearly, we can picture it for others more clearly. Receiving more life from God, and clear words and pictures to describe that life, we will be able to speak his message with more clarity and power.

ONE LORD, ONE FAITH

Before I go on talking about how this whole gallery of gospel images speaks to us, I want to make this clear: All these images and expressions are of the Christian gospel. By that I mean they talk about the life, death and resurrection of Jesus. The world doesn't need more fancy or even artful religious speech. No generic poetry about God will do, no matter how moving. "That which . . . we have seen with our eyes" is a definite reality, and his name is Jesus. He is our message, and we are not free to change it: "But even if we or an angel from heaven should preach a gospel other than the one we preached to you, let him be eternally condemned!" (Galatians 1:8).

Strong words, but good to remember as we think about speaking the gospel into a world that often rejects it. It is very tempting to change our message so that it becomes more pleasing. But we can't do this; we are bound by our Subject, the one we know and love. We must speak about him truly and hope that our hearers see the beauty in him that we do, and come to him to gain life.

Of course, there is no need to change the gospel or invent new ones to connect with our lives or those of our friends. Even at first glance, the richness of "every spiritual blessing in Christ" looks like it will provide fertile soil for as much expression as we would like. While the truth bends to no one, it has something to offer everyone.

THE APOSTLES' FOOTSTEPS

So we have a Savior who is the center of the gospel, and we have a gallery of images that show us who he is and what he has done for us. The New Testament authors have led the way for us. They have known him, let him work in their lives and then proclaimed this One they have come to know. So, to follow them in knowing and telling the gospel, we have to follow this path. We have to take these three steps: We have to let the gospel touch us, we have to rightly name the work of God in us as gospel, and then we can take that living and relevant word to our world.

Step 1: Experiencing the gospel. First, we must take the gospel in.

This happens when someone first becomes a Christian, but it also then begins to become a way of life. For example, one night I realized I was seeing a grown Christian man yelling at a seven-year-old girl. He was saying that she better not go rearrange those toys, and she was yelling back that oh yes, she would. Red-faced and loud-voiced, the man threatened physical punishment to the girl. Yes, that's how I found myself that evening, fighting with my daughter over what small plastic things did or did not belong to her. Somehow, in anger, I had moved out of parenting and into bullying. I sent us both to our rooms to cool down.

Ashamed by such behavior, I plopped down onto my bed and began to talk to God. But when I turned to him, acknowledging my sin, I found him telling me that I was already forgiven. I'd violated my position as father, made a mockery of manhood and ought to be given the boot. But I wasn't. He didn't drag me out like a criminal; he drew me near like a son. Now, to be honest, I did get a fatherly talking-to. But I was safe and accepted, even while I was reproved and corrected. (He does fathering right.)

So, ready to do better next time, I tried again. But it wasn't a week later that I lost my grip again, this time while helping with homework. I'd blown it, again. The hard truth was slowly becoming clear: I'm not completely in control of myself. Somehow anger had a grip on me. I couldn't beat it without help. So I prayed to my Savior for power to break the pattern I'd set over the years. I'd gotten myself into something I couldn't get out of—by myself at least. I needed rescue. And he has come, and over time he is showing me how to take on a new life with new patterns. When I'm about to pop off at one of my girls, he gives me freedom to step back, count to ten and react calmly. Someday, I am confident, he'll even grow the new life in me to the point where I can consistently use my anger well.

Step 2: Naming grace. Looking back on my story, I find myself naturally doing the same thing Paul did in Ephesians. In my life as a Christian, I see the many spiritual blessings in Christ, the many different sides of the gospel gift. And they come to me as different images of salvation.

In these situations with my daughter, I experienced the security of *sonship, rescue* from bondage and the gift of *freedom;* I recognize these now. I felt daily *forgiveness* and *new life* growing in me; now I know where they come from. This is not some nameless, generic grace given to those who once completed the gospel transaction. All these terms come from the gallery of gospel images. This is the gospel itself, working in my life today.

In fact, whenever I find myself rescued from some bad situation or habit, it is the power of Jesus' *salvation* that has lifted me. Whenever I experience release from sin or guilt or oppression, it is the *freedom* purchased by Jesus that I am experiencing. Whenever I know the homecoming welcome of the *Father,* I realize that it is the life and death of Jesus that is holding that door open for me. The richness of this gallery of gospel images drives home to me that all of the grace I know is found in Christ and that his grace is sufficient for me. My Christian life is the story of my ever-deepening experience of the gospel. I don't receive the gospel once and then move on to deeper teaching. My life's joy and work is to keep receiving, keep submitting to this wonderful gift. As Jesus said, "The work of God is this: to believe in the one he has sent" (John 6:29). And the whole gallery gives me great help and joy in that lifelong work.

This is how Paul described our job as disciples: "So then, just as you received Christ Jesus as Lord, continue to live in him, rooted and built up in him, strengthened in the faith as you were taught, and overflowing with thankfulness" (Colossians 2:6-7). My call as a disciple, as one who was once saved, is to allow the Savior to completely work out his salvation in me. I am to put down roots into that same gospel I received and to build my life squarely on it. The call is to travel deeper into the halls of his grace in Jesus, to learn from the images there of "every spiritual blessing in Christ" and to let that truth shape my life.

And a life full of the gospel will produce a gospel full of life.

Step 3: Proclaiming what we have seen and heard. So, I let the power of God touch my life, and I then name it as the power of God in Christ, as the work of the gospel. Now I have a lot more gospel to speak; as I experience all these blessings that flow from the cross, I have much more to say. And I can do it with conviction. When I talk with my neighbor Kurt about our lives and struggles, I don't have to begin back with my high school days to talk about God's power. I can take our lives right now, as dads, and talk about how Jesus gives me strength to get through the day.

I think back to that seminar I led and the students who came because they knew there had to be a better way to share the good news than what they had. I recall the student whose testimony was like a drawer-full of unlabeled and unorganized photos. Our speaking of the gospel doesn't have to be a rummaging around in the drawer of our life, sorting through unlabeled, generic God-experiences that we think only other Christians would understand. We can come to see all these experiences as blessings of the gospel; they all come through Jesus. So each of those experiences with God, seen through the Bible's gallery of images, can be a testimony of the gospel's power.

I think of the other students who reproduced their clean gospel outlines. They are no longer stuck with one outline that made sense at one point in their lives and occasionally becomes helpful again. They can now see all of their God-stories as gospel-stories. Knowing my whole life with God to be the work of the gospel in me, I now have a living and present Lord to speak of. Like a melody weaving its way through a piece of music, the truth of that outline, and more, weaves through my life, right up to today. I have every wonderful thing he has ever done for me, seen in light of the Bible's images, to speak as gospel. When I couldn't see how the gospel connected to most of my life, it was hard to speak it with clarity and power. But now, as the truth of these images becomes real in me, they can come out in my witness. I can now tell the many sides of God's good news to those who need it.

EVERY BLESSING MEETS EVERY NEED

As I see Jesus meet all my need, I can see how he meets the need of the whole world. The good news we know is good news for everyone. The various gospel images show how "every spiritual blessing in Christ" meets every spiritual need I have—and every need *we* have. I now have an entire gallery of images, of ways to proclaim Jesus. I can meet many people at many places, even if their lives and journeys are not like mine.

Being limited creatures, we can't hear all the sides of the gospel at once—even if we want to. We resonate with some part of it at first and then grow to understand more and more. And what strikes us first can be different from person to person. Now seeing the whole gallery, I don't have to bring people through the exact same understandings I had; an image of Jesus that I understood later may be the place where they first meet him. So, different images in the gallery not only fill more and more of my life with grace, they also can reach out to a variety of people.

I once had a classmate named Marissa with whom I was taking some public health classes. One day after class, as we talked over the problems of the world, she finally exclaimed, "So many of our systems are just broken and destructive. We need to change . . . everything! . . . the way whole nations work!"

I said, "I know. But no system is going to work right, if the people in it aren't good."

She eagerly leapt on this idea, "Yes! That's another real problem: the moral problem."

Right there, I could tell that Marissa was ready to hear about the kingdom of God. This is an image that Jesus took the lead in using, and Marissa was in a place to be reached by it. She knew that the whole world needed an overhaul, an overhaul that included a new people within it. If I had tried to show her a picture of God's work that dealt only with personal guilt and personal freedom, it would have been too small a picture. Forgiveness of the debt of personal sin would have sounded good, but it wouldn't have been enough to cover the evil she saw. Any solution for the world—and any Savior—would have to be world-sized. The kingdom of God is a picture that shows a new people in a new and just order, brought by someone big enough to make it work.

Bobby, on the other hand, was not in a place where he was looking at the whole world. He had a much sharper need, much closer to home.

Addicted to drugs, trying to get a degree and having to work his way through school—his life was a blur. As I spoke with him, his testimony was as run-on as his life seemed to be:

> Yeah, I would take speed to stay up all night and then I would go to class and then sometime in the afternoon I'd find myself driving to work, but I didn't even remember getting into the car but I had to go, I thought I probably had to work late that night—no wonder I was depressed at the same time I was running around like crazy. . . . I feel like I'm coming out of a fog.

We stood talking in the midst of a Christian group at his college that had loved and listened (and listened some more) to him. The picture he had gotten of Jesus was one of a kind Lord who had forgiven all his offenses and a strong Savior inside him who could break the grip of the addiction that held him. This was good news he could see he needed. These were vivid images that made sense of what his life was—and what it could be.

Knowing all the sides of the gospel, being familiar with that whole gallery of images, we can be confident that we have good gifts to give to any of our friends. Jesus really is good news for everyone we meet.

LETTING PICTURES BE PICTURES

So the gallery of gospel images calls deeply to each one who enters its halls, and it gives them much to say to their world. But the breadth of the collection is not only an opportunity; it's also a safeguard. It is not safe to use just one image alone, not even a favorite one.

We are presented with these images of Jesus, each showing some truth about him. Each of them has a role, a place where they excel and people to whom they speak most clearly. We'll see that much more as we go on and look at each image in detail. We should know at the start, though, that as each image has a strength, it also has limitations. As we go through this gallery of gospel images, we must keep in mind what we're doing. We are looking only at images. Each one is like a special mirror, catching one side of his glory. They show their nature as images by being two-dimensional. These are not the living truth in-the-round; they reflect the One who is. They catch one side of his glory, but they also have flat sides where they just don't help us. When we look at these images, we need to be as aware of their flat sides as we are of their clear messages.

One way to go wrong is to focus on just one image to build our life, our witness or our church around. If we do, we begin to think that the gospel is as limited as our one image of it is. We think of the gospel as ending where the image does. We get caught by the flat sides.

In my own story, the law court of God was a powerful image. One bad night as a teen, I was left alone to consider the mess I had made of my life. I felt my wrong weighing on me. I also felt a righteous God looking at me, and I had nothing to say. But when I gave up to him, I suddenly found that he wasn't counting all that foolishness and evil against me. I felt my justification in God's court well before I knew the theology behind it.

But the law court image is both wonderful and flat. I began to realize that while I was given God's stamp of approval, my life was still riddled with sin. And it wasn't going away very quickly. Would I always be actually rotten inside, even though my heavenly paperwork was in order? And I wasn't only uneasy about *me* seeing my sin; I knew God saw it too. I knew God sees people as they actually are. What did he *really* think of me? The Bible did say I would eventually become a better person, more pleasing to God. But was that as sure and certain, and as free, as the gospel?

But other images in the gallery reassured me, once I realized they were gospel too. I realized that he not only *justified* me in a legal sense but also put a new kind of *life* in me. He not only let me off the hook from his judgment but also *set me free* from the power of sin. Once an enemy, I was *reconciled* and *brought near*—I had not been left on my own to try to become good. The unmerited grace of God started me on the journey, and that "grace will lead me home." The rest of the gallery told me the rest of the story—and set my heart at ease.

THE GALLERY AND THE CALL OF JESUS

So the gallery of images guards us from errors that would eat away at our lives. It shows us the fullness of what God has done. It also shows us the fullness of what he will do as we follow him.

Remember Marissa, who was ready to hear the gospel portrayed as a call to God's kingdom? She would also have to realize things about following Jesus that the kingdom imagery is not strong on. Repenting from rebellious self-rule and bowing the knee to Jesus and his order is a beautiful way to start—but she'd need more help. There are deep internal changes required of a citizen of the kingdom. Images of the gospel as forgiveness and new life would come along and help her there.

And Bobby would learn that freedom from bondage was just a beginning of the gospel's call to him. The image of freedom, while sharp and clear, does not answer the question of "free for what?" The shape of freedom is described more in the sonship given us or the new way of the kingdom, which he did begin to embrace with passion. He wasn't free to do whatever he liked. He began to live for others and learn about how to serve the poor and oppressed; he took up a kingdom-shaped freedom.

So, once the gospel has gone deep in us and then gone out to others like Marissa and Bobby, it will go down deep in them also. And once the gospel is taken in and understood by them in turn, it will flow back out to others.

BOTH/AND

In this chapter, you've seen me switch back and forth between how the gospel speaks to Christians and how it speaks to those outside the church. I will keep on doing this throughout the book. This may bother you. You may want to know, "Is this a book about Christian growth or Christian mission?" I can only answer, "It is a book about the gospel." The gospel calls to us all. Christians cannot go out in mission if they are not growing in the gospel they are preaching, and that gospel will not come to anyone without calling them to a lifetime of growth in Jesus.

God is relentless in his drive to give everyone all the life they can possibly receive from him, and the gospel has not yet finished its work, even among God's people. I don't know any believers who are done learning how to believe. So the gospel is as much a call *to* the church as it is a call *from* the church. Christians and those outside the church are all called to the same table—the one Host satisfies all hungers. Our job as messengers is to call our neighbors to share the same cup and loaf that give us life. So, to be true to both you and the gospel, in these pages I can only show how he feeds us all. And the Bible's gallery of gospel images excels at showing his abundant provision for the whole world.

THE PRAISE OF HIS GLORIOUS GRACE

When that provision touches us and we come to know it, we sing his praises in all the language that God has given us in his Word. Listen to Athanasius, a fourth-century bishop and great defender of orthodoxy. Near the beginning of his classic *On the Incarnation*, he tries to succinctly summarize the work of Christ, but his language overflows, and he has to use a number of images from the gallery:

> Since it was necessary that the *debt* owing from sin should be paid again . . . he offered up his *sacrifice* also on behalf of all, he yielded up his temple to death in the stead of all, in order firstly to make men quit and free of their old *trespass*, and further to show himself *more powerful even than death*, displaying his body *incorruptible* as the *first fruits* of the resurrection of all.[4]

Like the apostles he followed, Athanasius was compelled by this amazing Savior to reach for the whole gallery of images to speak the gospel. And then, at the end of his book, after considering the wonder of what Jesus has done, he steps back to look at the work of this Savior and confesses he is speechless:

> In a word, the achievements of the Saviour, resulting from his becoming man, are of such a kind and number that if one should wish to enumerate them he may be compared to men who gaze at

the expanse of the sea and wish to count its waves. . . . All [his achievements] alike are marvelous, and wherever a man turns his glance, he may behold on that side the divinity of the Word, and be struck with exceeding great awe.[5]

"Exceeding great awe." This great father of the church knew well the value of words, defending the church against heresy, helping craft the Nicene Creed and facing several periods of exile for clinging to unpopular ways of preaching Jesus. But he didn't worship the words; instead, he used the words to worship Jesus and to lead others to worship him. Athanasius knew the deep awe that comes from seeing what God has done, and he engaged his mind to understand it. Having the experience of God's saving power and also having that rich biblical vocabulary to speak the gospel, he could stand up and speak with a power that changed his generation and left a mark on history.

If we could only see all these gospel images clearly and know how they preach the gospel to us! How much they could enrich our life, our witness and our praise. One Charles Wesley hymn exclaims, "O, for a thousand tongues to sing my great Redeemer's praise!" Just think—to be able to praise God in a thousand languages. Each of these images is like a language for expressing Jesus. And to speak about him truly is to praise him, because everything about him is excellent and wonderful.

When that praise is sung to those who are not in the Christian family, we call it witness. Seeing the whole gallery and knowing it clearly as a gallery of images that portray the gospel, we will have a powerful witness for the whole world.

THE GALLERY AS STUDIO

So here's our task: We need to become students of the New Testament authors, learning from their skill with these gospel images. We need to sit at the feet of these masters and learn to paint for our people as well as they painted for theirs. Our role is to be something like the students of art who go to the Louvre in Paris. Every day there you can see artists, young and old, sitting before works of the great masters with their pallets and their easels. They are learning by copying. They are taking in the greatness of the work before them and learning how to reproduce it. They want to be channels of that same kind of beauty. We need to get the art into us too, and we need to get it flowing out of us.

I saw these copyists in a magazine article and, even though I'd never met them, I was drawn in by their passion.[6] A retired maître d' was copying a Caravaggio because he was struck by the "palpitating beauty of the horse." I would've walked right by that painting; it wouldn't have made my heart race—at first. But this student of the masters could help me see a beauty I would never have appreciated otherwise.

Another painter was shown standing with a roomful of canvases, dozens of copies of masterpieces he had done. As he stood there with that roomful of images, I could see that he would have something to show anyone, no matter what they were interested in. I want to be that versatile and that able to connect with the people around me.

I was also drawn in by the intense concentration in the face of one young Californian artist as she worked at using the palette of the masterpiece before her. And I realized what was drawing me: the most fascinating thing about this copying process is not the paintings, but the painters. Time and time again as I saw photos of these copyists, I was drawn to them—the human artists. This process produces not only beautiful images but also captivating people, like the young woman who captivated that whole room with a simple and clear story of how God touched her life.

In our gospel gallery, the stories of Jesus are not the end product. That beauty transforms those who look at it and work with it; then they themselves become the work of art. You are to be the gallery. God's goal is an enormous hall full of living images of his truth, beauty and goodness. That will be a great witness to his glory. And true words will naturally come from his true people.

THE PROGRAM

So, in the following pages I am not going to be giving magic words to say. I am not going to show you how to assess your friends' need, show you how to pick an outline to match it and tell you how to deliver it so that they'll believe. What I will do instead is paint a number of these pictures clearly for you, so that you can get the gospel down deep in your mind and soul. I am going to show you how these images are good news for you and for the people in your world. In short, I am going to preach the gospel to you nine times over. By showing you the gospel through each of these nine images in turn, my hope is to sharpen your gospel vision, to build your gospel vocabulary.

After that guided tour through the work of the masters, I will give you a summary and some exercises as appendices. You can think of these as resources and lessons for aspiring art students.

My great hope is that, through more contact with this wonderful news, you will see and know the work of God more deeply in your life. Then it will be natural for a powerful gospel to come out of you. You will have engaging news that works today and great resources to help those around you hear God's call. In helping you be a deeper gospel-believer, I hope to help you be a better gospel-speaker. But first things first. The first word to eager disciples is "come and see."

So come and enter the gallery. Let it enter you. Jesus will show us who he is, and then we can sing it out to the world in a thousand languages.

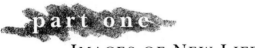

IMAGES OF NEW LIFE

I've chosen nine of the Bible's images of the gospel to show you in this book, in three groups of three. We'll see the gospel through the frameworks of these images of new life, images of mercy and restoration, and images of deliverance. (There are two kinds of people in this world—those who like charts and graphs, and those who don't. If you'd like to see the structure and content of this book summarized in a chart before you begin, go ahead and take a peek at appendix 1. If you'd rather take the experience as it comes, the chart will be waiting for you at the end, as a reminder of where you've been.)

I'm starting with three images of new life because these are the point of God's work in Jesus; he did all that he did so we might have new life. These images focus most strongly on what we were saved *for*.

Each image tells the whole story, the significance of the Lord's life, death and resurrection. If it didn't, it wouldn't be the gospel. Yet each image has strengths and weakness, places of focus and also flat sides. While each one tells the gospel story of God saving us from some bad thing and moving us into a good place, some focus on the saving-out-of side of things and some focus on the saving-into side. In other words, some major on what we are *saved from* and some on what we are *saved for*.

I want us to start with a focus on what we were *saved for* because it seems, in the end, the most important thing. It's God's goal, and ours. We are glad our enemies are defeated, so we can live in peace. We are glad our chains are broken, so we can live freely again.

The images of life, adoption and kingdom will tell us we have been saved out of some harsh realities. But their very names and vocabularies ring with a very positive promise, something worth moving forward for. So let's take a look and see what God has for us.

LIFE

Born from Above

A *man sits alone in his living room. He is healthy, successful, has a fine family—and is considering suicide. For him, every day is an agony of fear and doubt. If this is life, he wants out.*

A college junior cries alone in her dorm room. The burden of being a leader in her Christian group has become too much. What used to be joy for her has become painful, draining drudgery.

A leading citizen goes out alone, late at night, to the other side of town. Though he has everything, including religion, he's going to talk with a poor preacher, because he needs more.

What are these people crying out for? Life. The lives they have now aren't enough; they yearn for something more. So many people have stories like theirs, and Jesus can meet them in their need. The gospel speaks the language that these people need to hear. The New Testament calls it "this new life," "eternal life" or just "the life that is truly life," and offers it to us in Jesus (Acts 5:20; John 3:16; 1 Timothy 6:19).

This is the first gospel image we'll explore, so I thought I'd tell you what to expect as we get going. In order to let this image preach the gospel to us, I am going to let it really have its say. We'll focus on the vocabulary of life, letting it teach us with its distinctive voice. Like any of the images that weave through the Bible, it has a way of telling us the story of God and humanity—its own kind of light it sheds. So I'll spend some time pulling on just that thread from the Bible and let it work on our imaginations. Then we'll take what it has shown us and look at our lives, seeing how it can be good news for us and for our world.

We'll start with Jesus himself. He used this image in John 3 with that
leading citizen who came out at night, Nicodemus. Jesus saw that the
call and challenge of God would reach Nicodemus most clearly through
the idea of new life. Its language would call Nicodemus to see in a whole
new way, and it would show him the path he was missing. Though Nicodemus had it all in this life—respect, position, success, even morality
and religion—he still sought out this poor teacher at night. He was looking for something more.

> Now there was a Pharisee, a man named Nicodemus who was a
> member of the Jewish ruling council. He came to Jesus at night and
> said, "Rabbi, we know that you are a teacher who has come from
> God. For no one could perform the signs you are doing if God
> were not with him."
>
>   Jesus replied, "Very truly I tell you, no one can see the kingdom
> of God without being born again." (John 3:1-3 TNIV)

Nicodemus comes figuring that he is doing pretty well at seeking life:
"I know it when I see it." But Jesus tells him he has a far more desperate
need than he knows. Nicodemus was missing something so central that
he couldn't see God if he was sitting in front of him. Which, of course,
is exactly what was happening. Nicodemus needed radical help, a new
start, a birth from above that would let him see and move in a whole new
plane of existence. This was a little more drastic than Nicodemus was ex-
pecting, but listen as Jesus presses on.

> "How can anyone be born again when they are old?" Nicodemus
> asked. "Surely they cannot enter a second time into their mother's
> womb to be born!"
>
>   Jesus answered, "Very truly I tell you, no one can enter the king-
> dom of God without being born of water and the Spirit. Flesh gives
> birth to flesh, but the Spirit gives birth to spirit. You should not be
> surprised at my saying, 'You must be born again.' The wind blows
> wherever it pleases. You hear its sound, but you cannot tell where

it comes from or where it is going. So it is with everyone born of the Spirit." (TNIV)

"You should not be surprised." Why should Nicodemus not be surprised? Does it make perfect sense that something would break into his world and speak of a whole reality above it? That he should be called to a new and higher life? Apparently so. We should know that real life doesn't come from here. And this real life is so much higher than what we now have, if you don't have it yet, it's like you haven't yet been born.

Notice now how this surprising word blows in: "The wind blows wherever it pleases. You hear its sound, but you cannot tell where it comes from or where it is going." People often read this verse and then talk about how the Spirit is mysterious, like the wind. But this is not what Jesus is saying. It is not the Holy Spirit who is so mysterious here but "everyone born of the Spirit." They look like you, Nicodemus; they live in this world with you, but their life is from elsewhere. And they leave you wondering.

Jesus goes on to challenge Nicodemus further: "I have spoken to you of earthly things, and you do not believe; how then will you believe when I speak of heavenly things?" How can you grasp the life of heaven if you can't read the clues down here? Here, among earthly things, are signs that we were made for more. Life has come down to earth. Eternal life is moving among us, but remaining a mystery.

"Born again." The term has become so common Christians can forget that it speaks of this great mystery. Accepting Jesus is like stepping up to a whole new existence. What Jesus brings is like enough to what we are born with that we call it "life," yet it is also new, mysterious, eternal. Many people have the one, but are groping in the dark for the other. We are thinking, eating, breathing, working, yet we still need a truer, deeper life.

WAKING UP THIRSTY

Paul knew this. He, at least, was one Pharisee who understood how true life comes to our world—a world that is not as alive as it yearns to

be. This is how Paul, the reborn Pharisee, explained it to the people at
Athens:

> The God who made the world and everything in it is the Lord of
> heaven and earth and does not live in temples built by hands. And
> he is not served by human hands, as if he needed anything, be-
> cause he himself gives all men life and breath and everything else.
> (Acts 17:24-25)

God is not a part of your life, Paul was saying; he's the one with the
big life. The life you have now is part of a bigger plan.

> From one man he made all the nations, that they should inhabit
> the whole earth; and he marked out their appointed times in his-
> tory and the boundaries of their lands. God did this so that they
> would seek him and perhaps reach out for him and find him,
> though he is not far from any one of us. "For in him we live and
> move and have our being." As some of your own poets have said,
> "We are his offspring." (Acts 17:26-28 TNIV)

It's as if this world were a chessboard, and God set the pieces where
he wanted them to be, each in its place on earth and in the stream of history. But he has not put them there so that he might manipulate them all
by his own will. He has set each one in just the right place, the place
where it has the best chance to wake up to new life. God's goal is for
them to raise their eyes from the level of the chessboard, seek him and
perhaps reach out for him and find him. He has given us signs of real life
down here, heavenward-pointing "earthly things." He wants the
pieces—us, his offspring—to follow those clues. He wants them to wake
up, get real life from him and join the game.

We were given the lives we have in order to search for something
else. It's as if this life were a staging ground, a place to jump off into
"the life that is truly life." You could say this life is a two-dimensional
copy of a reality with depth or a vessel that waits to be filled. It's life,
but it's incomplete. We can think and feel, but one thing we feel is an

emptiness, a lack. It moves us to seek and reach out.

Justin, a friend of mine, had grown up as privileged as Nicodemus. He had all a young man could want, yet still he was a classic case of rich and unhappy. Wasn't there more to life? He went off to an elite university, and even in his years there he just couldn't find what he was looking for. Philosophy and religion classes, a bit of nightlife here and there—nothing filled the void. Somewhat depressed, he was sent off to travel Europe before his senior year. Not much to pity about his life . . . except that he was wasting away inwardly.

"God did this so that they would seek him." It's as if we woke up thirsty for something we've never known. And while we make do with whatever we can find down here, we keep coming across clues about a spring that will truly satisfy. When we notice one of these clues in our earthly life, it awakens our hope for something more. And, like Nicodemus, we move off in search of it. But where to look?

SPEAKING OF EARTHLY THINGS

Jesus said to Nicodemus, "I have spoken to you of earthly things, and you do not believe." Nicodemus, there are realities right in front of you, facing you in this life, that tell you about what God has for you. But you aren't putting it together. Paul says the same thing to the Athenians: Look! Can't you tell that the Author of all life is right there, waiting to be found by you? The clues are there for us too, but in the crazy mix of this life, how do we find them?

In the house next door we have an overflow of life: a three-year-old, a one-year-old and new twin boys. We are often happily surrounded by youthful energy and small plastic toys. And that's just when they visit us for brief periods. You should see *their* house. That's life.

And life struck me in a magazine that I picked up last summer. I opened it and saw a picture of a friend, one I remember meeting as a college freshmen in a messy dorm room. But he has grown up a bit. In the photo he now wears the uniform of an Army captain as he moves wounded soldiers from a helicopter. Life goes there too.

Then I remember standing silent as an old Marine was laid to rest, with two aged veterans, ramrod straight, serving as honor guard. The Marine was my uncle, who saw action on Iwo Jima. He carried that war inside, never speaking of it, for decades after. What of his life?

No wonder the poets (from the time of the ancient Greeks till today) have been kept constantly busy with this wild mix we call life. Love, death, sorrow, beauty, pain—it's all flying around in a dizzying storm. And there are signs in among these earthly things, facing us as we stand in our set places and times. They call us to "reach out for him and find him." We hear the sound but cannot tell where it comes from or where it is going.

THIS LIFE—YES AND NO

Seeking higher life is an old pursuit. Christian tradition (and all the major religions) have two basic responses to the life we are given in this world. As we seek like Nicodemus, religions show us two different ways of sorting through this life to find "the life that is truly life." They are the way of affirmation and the way of negation—saying yes to this life or saying no to it.

Those who affirm this life see signs of real life in the world. They find the good that is here and see God's truth in it. You could call these the spiritual romantics. They take a walk in the woods and see the Creator's hand. They hear a symphony and wonder at the God-given ability of humans to create beauty. They do a satisfying day's work and rejoice that they can provide for others with the hands God gave them. They say yes to this life in its goodness.

Those pursuing the way of denial see the world too. They see how its beauty distracts us from true beauty and how there is nothing in human society that is not twisted. These are the monks and mystics, for whom this life is a trap. Thomas à Kempis says to his students in *The Imitation of Christ*, "As often as I have been among men, I have returned home less a man."[1] He sees how the world's games pull us down. The way of negation warns us that seldom do people see worldly blessings and think beyond them to the Creator. Instead we too often set our hearts on created things, settling for treasures on earth. For the monks, mystics and ascetics, the world is a veil to be pushed aside. They say no to it, so that they may say yes to the ultimate good of God.

THE LIFE APPEARED

In one place the two streams come together in a very concrete way, pointing to the same sign. There is a clear point where they both say, "Real life is seen here." It is in the person of the hero or heroine. Whether they are heroes of ancient myths or modern comic books, a good rousing story or a movie, these figures share the same defining marks. And they are recognized by both our ways of sorting through this life, the way of affirmation and the way of negation.

Heroes are the pinnacle of the affirmation of life. They are full of life; we call them "larger than life." They are powerful and smart and good. (Often they even get to be good-looking.) Who hasn't dreamed of being a hero?

But how do they affirm life? Through denial. They say no to the unjust world order. They champion the weak against those who misuse power. And they not only say no to the twistedness of life here, they often say no to their own life. Time and again, in order to be the hero they say no to their own happiness, their own freedom and often their very lives.

This is the mark of the hero, from Spider-Man ("With great power comes great responsibility") to Frodo Baggins ("I tried to save the Shire, and it has been saved, but not for me")[2] to Jesus ("For even the Son of Man did not come to be served, but to serve, and to give his life as a ransom for many"; Mark 10:45). Yes, Jesus. Jesus may be more than a hero, but he certainly is no less. Heroes are heroes because they give their great lives for others. Who fills these shoes better than Jesus? They are his, after all. Every hero I have ever loved, I have loved because they look like Jesus. He's the one, the mold, the archetype.

If any hero affirms life, Jesus does so even more. We simply wake up here, in the places and times set for us. We didn't choose to have this life;

all of a sudden we just find ourselves here. We see what's good and wonderful, and if we are brave we set out to preserve it. But Jesus loves and affirms this life even more. First, he helped create all that we have ever seen and loved. And then, not only did he make it, he also chose to step into it, to take up our life in this world. We simply find ourselves on the chessboard. He consciously chose it, stepping down onto the board with us. Then, think about the life he lived when he got here. Who has been bolder or stronger or more wise and compassionate? As he walked among us, he was full to the brim with the good life of God.

If he affirmed life more strongly than anyone we have seen, he also denied it more decisively. He took on all that is evil and oppressive here. Lies, demons, illness, sin and death—he said no to all un-life. And he did it by taking his great life and pouring it out for us. His life was good and beautiful, but he was willing to deny it in order to bring even more life to us all.

That's a hero. That's a life. If there was something I wanted to be, it would be that. That's what I woke up thirsty for. That's what I went off in search of, even though I didn't know what I was looking for. Seeing that life, I want to raise my eyes above the level of this life and reach out for more. I would want to be near the people who had it. I would try to imitate them so I could have what they have. This is what I need, not just in my world but down deep in myself. His life is the life I need in me.

To point to this man, the bringer of true life, is to proclaim the gospel. The message of the cross is God's life given for ours, and his life given to us. And what he has to give is the real thing. Listen to John: "The life appeared; we have seen it and testify to it, and we proclaim to you the eternal life, which was with the Father and has appeared to us" (1 John 1:2). We point to Jesus and say, "He is the life." The gospel is a call to acknowledge him as the source of true life . . . and to come to him and receive it. For the life he has, he has in order to give to us.

THE DEMANDING BEAUTY

What does it mean to be born from above? What does it take? In John's prologue it seems so simple: "Yet to all who received him, to those who believed in his name, he gave the right to become children of God—children born not of natural descent, nor of human decision or a husband's will, but born of God" (John 1:12-13).

Simple, but not easy. Here we come to an element in this telling of the gospel that we will find in them all. All these images have what I will call a "demanding beauty." They are wonderful, but if we are to really take them in, it will cost. If you are really going to study one of the great masterworks, you need to turn your attention to it, giving it your time and effort. In the way that all students must, you must submit: you need to allow it to set the terms by which you understand it. And ultimately, if it is to be of any use or be a lasting part of you, you need to take it into your heart and mind.

Any image of the gospel will make these demands on us. The gospel is offered freely, yet we must respond. One word for this is *repentance;* we must turn away from what holds us back and turn to God. The language of life, as positive as it is, is no exception. If something is in the way of this new life, we must get rid of it.

Think again of Nicodemus. What did he find when he came to Jesus? He came saying, "We know . . . " and Jesus stopped him cold: "No, you don't know. No one can see the kingdom, unless he is born from above." Nicodemus had come with all the fruit of his mature earthly life. He knew about God. He was part of the religious elite—"*We* know." He had figured out where Jesus had come from, or so he thought. And he came to have a private talk—one enlightened person to another—to get a last bit of revelation to top off his tank.

But Jesus would not leave him in his illusion, the illusion that the life he had was enough: Nicodemus, you can't even *see* the kingdom unless you have a whole new life. You think you know where I come from— you can say the word *God*—but you have no idea where I come from or where I am going. You must be born again.

Here we have come to the demanding beauty of this image of the gospel. To take up the new life, we are called to let go of our old one. Think of Nicodemus hearing that he must be born again. He already had life. He had a full, rich and respected life. If it wasn't quite enough, it still was as good as it gets down here. And all of that must be given up and a new start made. A lot is offered in this call of the gospel, but a lot is also required.

THROUGH DEATH TO LIFE

Nicodemus is not alone. Everyone who comes to Jesus for life hears the same call. Peter and the disciples had come to Jesus because they sensed that life was there. And they brought with them their ideas about what life was. So when Peter names Jesus as the Messiah, the chosen one of the living God, he has visions of the ascendant and affirmed hero of God. But then Jesus explains his life, and his life plan, to the disciples: he is the one who would save his people by suffering and dying for them.

And Peter tells him off. The Messiah and (of course) his followers should be winners, not losers. Pain and death are for the bad guys. Peter does not want a share in the life of a suffering servant. He wants a celebrity's life, not a hero's. But Jesus insists,

> "If any want to become my followers, let them deny themselves and take up their cross and follow me. For those who want to save their life will lose it, and those who lose their life for my sake, and for the sake of the gospel, will save it. For what will it profit them to gain the whole world and forfeit their life?" (Mark 8:34-36 NRSV)

Jesus was adamant that his life was to be given away; that was his path to glory. And if anyone was to get life from him, they needed to follow the trail he blazed. Let go of your life to receive the new life God will give you. There is no other way.

A CONVERSION OF LIFE

This dying to self to find life in God is not some advanced lesson of Christianity, it is a way of speaking the gospel. To say "lose your life so that you might save it" is the way this image speaks "repent and believe."

Does that mean that God asks new believers to be immediately ready to die for his cause as a condition of getting life? No, but they must accept a kind of death. Listen to Paul as he talks about baptism, the very beginning of this new life:

> Don't you know that all of us who were baptized into Christ Jesus were baptized into his death? We were therefore buried with him through baptism into death in order that, just as Christ was raised from the dead through the glory of the Father, we too may live a new life. (Romans 6:3-4)

The reality of having to lose life in order to save it is there at the start. The very act of saying yes to the life of Jesus means saying no to mine.

When C. S. Lewis describes "mere Christianity," he talks about the dying that starts our new living:

> This process of surrender—this movement full speed astern—is what Christians call repentance. Now, repentance is no fun at all. It is something much harder than merely eating humble pie. It means unlearning all the self-conceit and self-will that we have been training ourselves into for thousands of years. It means killing a part of yourself, undergoing a kind of death. . . . This repentance, this willing submission to humiliation and a kind of death, is not something God demands of you before he will take you back and which he could let you off if he chose: it is simply a description of what going back to him is like.[3]

Accepting death in order to receive life. Do you see how this first step of humble repentance is a bit like the great heroic act of Jesus? Even that first step—denying life in order to gain it—is an evidence of the new life: it shows the character of Jesus beginning to be formed in us. After that tiny first spark of new life, the newly "born again" begin to grow into that life. The rhythm of dying to self and living in God, like the out-then-in rhythm of breathing, becomes the pattern of our new lives.

Now, God does not expect new believers to give up their lives for others on the spot (though some have), any more than you'd expect a baby to walk into the kitchen and fix dinner. But you do expect it to nurse, get strong, and grow. The point is that a particular kind of life is growing from the start. That is the life seen in Jesus, the "eternal life, which was with the Father." It is the life that lives by giving itself away. That is the life we are called to in the gospel—God's very own, which he shares with us in Jesus.

GOOD NEWS

So we are called to get new life from God then to spend these lives here on others, like Jesus did. And when they are all spent, we are promised a share in the unending and glorious life of Jesus. But even now, between that first cry in the birthing room and our full maturity, that new life is growing. Like Jesus, we will face many little deaths: self-denials, humiliations and sufferings that we can take as chances for the new life to grow. Paul looks at the hardships he faces for the sake of others and sees life there:

> We are hard pressed on every side, but not crushed; perplexed, but not in despair; persecuted, but not abandoned; struck down, but not destroyed. We always carry around in our body the death of Jesus, so that the life of Jesus may also be revealed in our body. . . . Therefore we do not lose heart. Though outwardly we are wasting away, yet inwardly we are being renewed day by day. (2 Corinthians 4:8-10, 16)

This is the gospel of life. The true life appeared in Jesus, the kind of life that denies itself for others and so becomes even greater than before. We are called to accept his life, his way, and leave ours. We are called to say no to a life we will lose anyway and say yes to his kind of life. Then the Spirit will come and kindle in us the life of Jesus. We are given the promise that his life will grow in us amidst all the suffering here. And we are promised that his life will outlast all that, leap through death and then continue to run on free forever.

This is good news. It is good news to those who, in the process of trying to save their lives, feel them slipping away. It is good news to those who feel the limits of this life, who feel the sting of death slowly taking effect. Those who feel the creeping presence of death, in all its forms, need this word.

So we have taken our look at this great story through this lens, this image. Now we'll turn to look at some ways this news goes out and meets the people it was made for. While this is just one image, when we let it speak the gospel it meets many people and many needs.

DIVINE DISCONTENT

New life is good news for restless seekers. I earlier mentioned Justin, my privileged but empty friend. He felt he was without real life, but he was not without real friends who could point the way for him. One had invited him to visit a certain community while he was in Europe. It was L'Abri in Switzerland, founded by Francis and Edith Schaeffer, a place with life to offer.

Justin went, and he found a community that was brimming with real life. It was alive with love and hospitality, alive with humanity that worked and prayed and sang. And it talked; it was also alive intellectually. It was more real, true and alive than anything he had seen before. These people not only experienced the new life, they also understood it in its fullness and could speak of it. The words of life rang out from them with the clarity and power that comes from truth lived. And my friend was born from above in that place.

How many people's stories are variations on this theme? So many people around us are wandering and searching. They might swing from partner to partner or business venture to business venture or thrill to thrill, yet they never find what satisfies. They need to hear that there is a true life to be had, that there is a reason everything in this life just does not satisfy us. Remember, Paul said, "We are his offspring." We were made for God and will always be restless away from the one in whom "we live and move and have our being" (Acts 17:28).

Seekers need to hear about life from those convinced of it, those who are full of the new life. But how often do I, a person born from above, look like someone who has been filled from above? Or do I more often act like a desperate seeker for life? How often do I drive down the road, preoccupied with how my life would be nicer if I drove a new car—like that one there? Time and again, I find myself acting like any other frantic consumer. If I can just take in a few more goods and services, my life will be full and rich, right?

And if possessions don't fill me up, I can try consuming people. That sounds ugly, I know, but I need to be honest: if I don't get life from above, I have to get it somewhere. I can gather friends around me and live off their approval. I can try to fill up on the love of that one special someone. I can try hard to walk out of every meeting or party with a harvest of admiration and respect.

Too often, though I have been born from above, I can't bear to completely repent, to completely give up on my old strategies for seeking life. Too often I'm not breathing out the life of heaven; I'm straining to suck in the life of earth. I desperately pull things and people into my orbit. I look like someone who is playing the game to save his own life. If I only believed my own gospel! Jesus is not only the one source of life after death, he's also the only one who can get me any life worth having.

SERVING DEATH

Let's consider another person who needs a word of life. Remember that college junior, sobbing in her dorm room? Sherrie was a Christian leader, but where was the life? She had accepted the gospel and was doing what Jesus said. She was serving, living out "you-not-me" all the time. She was dying to self in order to find new life, but it wasn't working. She felt like she was just plain dying.

As we talked it out, she realized she lived by putting others ahead of herself, even before Jesus had called her. Her family was full of brokenness, and she had always been the one to keep the family functioning. Serving them and keeping the peace was a survival strategy—being "the good one" was a way of saving her life. Later, church groups found her habits very useful. But saving her life this way was killing her. Could she let it go? Could she let that gospel of life, which she had once received, go even deeper? Could she turn to Jesus for life again? Could she die to live, stop frantically trying to be a good Christian—so she could be a better one? It would be a kind of death, to leave her old strategies, her ways of building her own life.

I watched her take the next step in that gospel journey, letting the life of Jesus fill her at a new level. And I pray for her now, years later, as she raises a family of her own. I know she will struggle with taking in that life deeper and deeper as she faces the temptation to make her own life rather than receive his. Receiving the gospel of life every day is her only hope.

THE BLANK WALL

The sting of death is not always so subtle. We can go for long periods playing the game of saving life, but the stark reality of death will not be denied. Perhaps there is a hard mercy here; death makes us wake up and face the limit of this life. But can we face it? Is all this metaphorical talk of life still good news in the face of real death, the death of our bodies?

Mary and Martha believed in Jesus and his words, to a point. They knew he could handle some of the more spiritual or smaller forms of death. In John 11, we read that they believed he could have healed their brother. As Martha said, "If you had been here, my brother would not have died." But these believers, deep down, believed that nothing could deal with that ultimate wall, death. However, Jesus did not acknowledge that limit. He had a bigger life in himself. "I am the resurrection and the life."

At the graveside of my father-in-law, I had to speak the gospel of life. I was looking into the faces of those who were in the middle of their grief, speaking right over the box that held his body. And the thought spun through my mind, *All this had better be true.*

Can we believe that the life of Jesus is more real than death? Facing the last wall, can we hold on to the word of life? If we can, we have an amazing word to speak to those who grieve and fear. Our culture sends them to the graveside alone. But Jesus comes with them, weeps with them, and brings them life.

> Since the children have flesh and blood, he too shared in their humanity so that by his death he might destroy him who holds the power of death—that is, the devil—and free those who all their lives were held in slavery by their fear of death. (Hebrews 2:14-15)

If we believe the gospel, death holds no fear for us anymore, and it puts this life in such good perspective. Where there once were only whisperings of dread, there now can be openness and freedom. We can admit the game board is only so big. We've got a certain amount of time here to do some good, then on with Life: Part Two. Turning death into a part of the good news? That's a powerful word.

IN THE WILDERNESS

Who else needs the word of life? Those who feel death's bite in the form of despair. Despair sees the limit of life, and nothing else. It sees the dead end with no hope of a good road ahead. Helen told me her story of facing just such a dead-end. Her life was wrapped up in a relationship with a horrible boyfriend, whom she had come to loathe. As she looked ahead, life seemed so bleak she was seriously considering suicide. Then a novel thought occurred to her, one that changed everything: "I could just leave him."

Now she laughs when she recalls how simple the step to hope was, how simple to gain a whole new vision of her life. It seemed so obvious to those outside the box she was in. But how many of us are often trapped in the boxes of life here? Those boxes are not always so easy to step out of. In my time in campus ministry I have talked to too many students, supposedly with their whole lives ahead of them, who are trapped in depression. There seems nothing worth doing or nothing they can do. And the walls close in. This past year, on just one campus in our area, seven students ended their own lives.

My friend Ben was at just such a place. He was a believer, even a Christian teacher, on whom the walls were closing in. The effort of saving his own life was too much. Building an unassailable image through work and a friendly personality—staving off fear through pleasing people—had just become too shaky and too painful.

But God meets people in the wilderness, in the place where life seems impossible. That was the time and place he met Hagar, after Abraham had sent her away (see Genesis 21). At the end of her strength in the desert, she set her baby boy down and waited to die. But God came. He brought water in the desert and a promise of many generations of life through her son, Ishmael. God broke in with life. He made "a way out of no way."

As Ben faced his desert time, sitting in his living room alone, he looked up and saw a picture of his wife and children. Something moved in him; he couldn't leave them alone in the world. I know what that "something" was. What would move a man to give up his release from great pain so that he might live to serve others? What would move a man to such a brave act that would be so costly? It was eternal life, making its characteristic you-not-me step. It was the life and Spirit of Jesus. Those born of the Spirit move in strange ways; they even choose pain so they can find a greater life on the other side.

So Ben swallowed his pride, faced his pain and made the call for help. And the move of following Jesus into that death has reaped so much more life. He has moved more and more away from saving his own life into giving it away for his wife and children. And he is becoming more and more a man full of freedom and joy. Would you be surprised to hear that this life is spilling over into his family? A spring of living water is what Jesus promised, and it's true.

Life is a true way to speak the gospel, to say who Jesus is and what he has won for us. He brings true life. It begins to fill those who follow him. They begin to breathe joy, purpose and hope. And he sends them out into his world to be living signs of the true life.

That is good news.

ADOPTION

Chosen in Love

Life is a powerful way to speak the gospel, but it does have limits. Its strength leads to one of its flat sides. It is very strong and primal, but because of this it is not very specific. What does *life* mean, and what does it look like? What is the nature and character of this life? Simply put, what kind of life are we getting?

The image of adoption by God answers this question. We are being welcomed into God's household to live with him as his Son does. We are being given the kind of life the Son of God has. This is a call to come inside, to come into God's family, and it can be just the word that many need to hear.

My friend Lee needed this badly. You could see it in his face: he was an "angry young man." His story is so familiar, it would be boring if it weren't so real. Lee's father was harsh, violent and unpredictable—when he was around at all. By the time Lee turned sixteen, he had decided to do life his own way; no more relying on unreliable people, no more letting people hurt him. Through the hard times, his mother had become a Christian, but Lee was done with having other people tell him what to do. As he sat in the church youth group that his mother dragged him to, his face was a mask as he listened to the preacher talk. Yeah, sure, people are sinners, the world is a mess—that was no news to him. As they talked of God and salvation, Lee sat there wondering what the angle was, what these nice people really wanted. At the same time, his youth group leader was wondering how the gospel could break through to Lee. What would be good news to this hard young man?

Julie, on the other hand, was a young woman who didn't seem to need any radical good news. When she walked onto her college campus, she didn't look like a classic candidate for conversion. She was a kind person, had good morals and did well in school. But she met some Christians on campus and was drawn into the fellowship's orbit. What she found there was a whole new level of friendship and love. She experienced a kind of welcome that she never knew she had been missing. As she spent more time with this community, she began to realize that she wanted more. She didn't want to stay as a guest—as nice as that was. She wanted to be in, really in. Meanwhile some of her Christian friends were thinking about her, wondering what to say next. What did Julie need? What was her next step?

Both of these very different people were experiencing the same gospel. They were hearing God's call to become part of his family; the gospel was coming to them as the welcome of the Father. What they needed to do was drop everything else and accept his welcome.

The Bible gives a rich, clear picture of the gospel as adoption, sonship and inheritance. If we can keep our ears open for terms like *Father*, *Son*, *children* and *heirs*, they will put together for us a picture of being welcomed home in Jesus. It's a picture many of us need. George MacDonald, a Scottish preacher who was a great inspiration to C. S. Lewis, said, "The refusal to look up to God as our Father is the central wrong in the whole human affair; the inability [to look up to God], the one central misery."[1]

Having said this, MacDonald realized—even in 1867—that many of us have painful associations with fatherhood:

> There may be among my readers—alas for such!—to whom the word Father brings no cheer, no dawn, in whose heart it rouses no tremble of even a vanished emotion. It is hardly likely to be their fault. . . . Therefore I say to the son or daughter who has no pleasure in the name Father, "You must interpret the word by all you have missed in life. . . . All that human tenderness can give or de-

sire in the nearness and readiness of love, all and infinitely more must be true of the perfect Father—the maker of Fatherhood."[2]

Just as we often know about eternal life from what we feel of its lack, perhaps we can let the feeling of all we have missed in earthly fatherhood move us to search for the Father we know must be there. In the hope that he will meet you with that word, either in your good or bad past, I am going to follow this image in the Bible and call him Father, and hope that will serve you well.

THE EXTRAVAGANT FATHER

Something about God made Jesus very ready to call him Father. He taught us it was good—and safe—to think of him that way. His story of the father and the lost sons in Luke 15 is a good starting place, a first look at this Father and his heart for us.

> There was a man who had two sons. The younger one said to his father, "Father, give me my share of the estate." So he divided his property between them.
>
> Not long after that, the younger son got together all he had, set off for a distant country and there squandered his wealth in wild living. After he had spent everything, there was a severe famine in that whole country, and he began to be in need. So he went and hired himself out to a citizen of that country, who sent him to his fields to feed pigs. He longed to fill his stomach with the pods that the pigs were eating, but no one gave him anything.
>
> When he came to his senses, he said, "How many of my father's hired men have food to spare, and here I am starving to death! I will set out and go back to my father and say to him: Father, I have sinned against heaven and against you. I am no longer worthy to be called your son; make me like one of your hired men." So he got up and went to his father.
>
> But while he was still a long way off, his father saw him and was filled with compassion for him; he ran to his son, threw his

arms around him and kissed him.

The son said to him, "Father, I have sinned against heaven and against you. I am no longer worthy to be called your son."

But the father said to his servants, "Quick! Bring the best robe and put it on him. Put a ring on his finger and sandals on his feet. Bring the fattened calf and kill it. Let's have a feast and celebrate. For this son of mine was dead and is alive again; he was lost and is found." So they began to celebrate.

The son's behavior here is outrageous ("Dad, I just want your money. Give me my cut, and I'm gone"). But to Jesus' hearers, the Father's behavior would have been even more shocking. Respect for parents and elders was more highly valued in their culture than it is in ours. And here this son had shamed his father and rejected him. That ungrateful wretch had disgraced his family and his community. Then he had the gall to come home again. But when he came home, the father threw his dignity to the wind and ran out to greet him. His son had wasted all he had been given, but the father embraced him and gave him more of the best. This son was a family disgrace, but the father made him the guest of honor.

This joyfully extravagant Father was in Paul's mind as he wrote to the Ephesians,

> Praise be to the God and Father of our Lord Jesus Christ, who has blessed us in the heavenly realms with every spiritual blessing in Christ. For he chose us in him before the creation of the world to be holy and blameless in his sight. In love he predestined us to be adopted as his sons through Jesus Christ, in accordance with his pleasure and will. . . . In him we have redemption through his blood, the forgiveness of sins, in accordance with the riches of God's grace that he lavished on us with all wisdom and understanding. (Ephesians 1:3-5, 7-8)

We've seen this verse before and looked at how various images work together in it to give us a full picture of the gospel. Now let's look at the central image here: adoption. This Father gives "every spiritual blessing," and he does so in love. It was his good pleasure, his determination, that we should be his children. He calls us this, even though we come back to him with a load of sin, because he wants to lavish his grace on us. Paul is painting a picture of the Father that he has learned from Jesus.

His portrait is like the Luke 15 story in another way too. Ancient Roman readers would not think first of the adoption of a tiny infant, but of a prominent man adopting a young adult to be his heir. This adoption signals not only love but also approval and the gift of a life with a future.

A PURPOSED LOVE

These images bring the Father into clear view, and what we see is him acting decisively to make us his. Some human parents are surprised by—even dragged into—parenthood, but not this Father. He is more than active; he is exuberant, lavish and . . . determined. His love is wildly generous and passionately felt, and yet settled and deep. He chose us well in advance, and he loves us with "wisdom and understanding."

The picture of adoption highlights his choice to give us all his gifts. This choice is very real to me, as an adopted child myself. I wish I could tell you of my great feelings of loneliness before my parents brought me home—but I was only nine months old and not very deep yet. I learned the story of my adoption when I was twelve, and my imagination eagerly went to work on this new truth: they picked me. They went to that orphanage back in Providence, Rhode Island, walked in, came up to my crib, smiled at me and said, "We want him."

Now, I am ashamed to say that there were times when I used this image to mentally one-up my naturally acquired siblings: Mom and Dad got stuck with them, but they *picked* me. But that wasn't too often. Mostly I just felt like their child. I was theirs because they wanted me to be.

COMING HOME

How does Jesus' story of the prodigal fit in, then? Aren't we talking about a natural son there? We are, yet this picture is closer to that of adoption than we often think, and it also adds something very important. That younger son had given up his place as a son; he had no more rights at home. What the father did in greeting him and giving him the ring and the robe was far more than dressing him—he was giving him back his place as son. He went from being dead to the family to being at its heart.

This story is important to keep close to the idea of adoption. Adoption shows a father taking an outsider and making that person his child. But Jesus' story of the prodigal highlights something about that outsider: he is brought not only to God's home but also to his own.

Before God comes for us, we are lost in a foreign country with no way home and no one to care for us. In an important way, we are not his children—we are completely estranged from him. We are dead to God, gone from the household, stripped of all rights; yet we *are* his and we know it, however dimly. We were made in his image, and it still marks us. We know that we were made to be loved, even if we don't always know how or by whom. So when God claims us as his own, we are not going to some alien place where we don't belong; we are going to the home we've always longed for, the place we were made for, the home that has been waiting for us.

My friend Trish once told me (with a brilliant smile), "Oh, yeah, in college I had no idea who I was. I slept around and all that gross stuff. But now I'm . . . right where I belong." Someplace she had never been before—in God's family—was right where she belonged. And being home was suiting her well.

That's why we have images of both adoption and homecoming. They show us that the Father is doing a radical new thing, publicly giving us all the security and rights of the household, and they show us that we are being brought home. The great thing to see in both images is the Father and his amazing welcome.

COMING TO OUR SENSES

The images seem clear enough, and they can be very inviting. But what does it mean to step into this picture? How can we accept this love?

Looking back at that wayward son can help us see our way home. His path back to the Father can show us something of our own way home.

In Jesus' story we can see clearly the love of this Father. We can hardly see much else. Yet this is the Father that the younger son left. This love and rich provision is what he abandoned. What was he thinking?

He wasn't. Jesus clearly thinks what the prodigal did was insane, out of touch with reality. What he says about the turnaround was that this son "came to his senses." What was this new, sane thought that came to him? *Of course! I have a Father who will care for me.* In turning to his father, he returns to himself. Even at this turning point though, he didn't truly understand his father. He assumes that he will find a grudging welcome and a business deal—work for bread. He doesn't yet know that coming home is enough. He doesn't know that, of all his prepared speech, all he really needs to say is "Father."

This is a clue to the sanity of coming home, the clue to what we sinners need. The sinner says, "Here I am, grubbing around in all this muck and barely surviving. But God will take me in. Why don't I go to him?" This life-saving thought, this sweet voice of reason, is not something that we come up with on our own. It blows in from elsewhere. It is sanity borrowed from someone else. As Paul wrote, "For you did not receive a spirit of slavery to fall back into fear, but you have received a spirit of adoption. When we cry, 'Abba! Father!' it is that very Spirit bearing witness with our spirit that we are children of God" (Romans 8:15-16 NRSV). Our ragged and starved spirits are in no shape to make the trip home, but the Spirit of Jesus comes to our spirits and lifts them up. We come to our senses in Jesus. The Spirit, the sanity of the true Son, comes to us and enables us to say, "Father," just as he does.

He knew how to cry, "Abba! Father." From beginning to end he knew how to turn his face toward God. The eternal Son had taken a human life then lived it in perfect sonship and gave it to an unworthy world. He trusted his Father to the very end, saying, "Father, into your hands I commit my spirit" (Luke 23:46). And the Father saw this perfect Son and approved. He called him home. Jesus was "his son, who as to his human nature was a descendant of David, and who through the Spirit of holiness was declared with power to be the Son of God" (Romans 1:3-4). And this perfect Son sends to us his Spirit, the Spirit of adoption, to lead us home.

HEARING HIS VOICE

Here's another way to picture receiving this welcome into God's family, a simple way to sum up this good news of adoption. Jesus first appeared publicly when John was baptizing. All the people were going out and confessing their sins. Being baptized was like saying to God, "We are unworthy; have mercy on us." Jesus comes in obedience like all the rest. He is among them, doing what they do, but quite a different word is said about him. The Father speaks from heaven, "You are my son, whom I love; with you I am well pleased" (Mark 1:11). Then Jesus goes off to live and die so all of us can hear those words.

Now Jesus stands among sinners, as he did at his baptism. He stands among those he died to call brothers and sisters. Now we can walk over to him, look up and hear along with him, "You are my daughters and sons, whom I love. With you I am well pleased." And our spirits can now respond, "Father."

ALL THE WAY IN

"How great is the love the Father has lavished on us, that we should be called children of God! And that is what we are!" (1 John 3:1). John is rightly amazed, because he knows how deep this welcome is. A soul with a grip on this truth will speak it with amazement and joy and wonder, with the power and clarity it deserves.

I wonder if I can make you feel the significance of this from my story, but I will try. I said that when I was told at twelve that I had been adopted, I began to imagine how my parents chose me. But that was not my first reaction. My first thought was, *Wow, I'm adopted. I'm not really theirs. This is big.* But after just a moment I realized I didn't feel different at all. Nothing was different. My mom was sitting in the car with me, just having told me this and, when we were ready, she would drive me home and make dinner for us, like always. This big-deal thing didn't really make any difference at all.

Now, of course the fact of my adoption made all the difference; it gave me that mother and father and that whole life. But what struck me was that being adopted made no difference *to my being their child.* I was their kid and that was that. There was nothing my siblings had that I didn't. No one had a clue I was adopted. I was all the way in. I had thought adoption meant something less than really being in. But it turns out that adoption is just another way to have a child that is really yours.

We are really God's children. We are not neighborhood children fondly allowed to play in the front yard. In John 14, Jesus tells his friends, "In my Father's house are many rooms; if it were not so, I would have told you. I am going there to prepare a place for you." The Son has prepared a place for us in the household, in the very heart of God. We are let all the way in.

THE DEMANDS OF SANITY
But do we want in? This image of the gospel also has a demanding beauty. Some things must happen in us if we are to step into this great welcome.

Here I want to stop and point out something that is true of the call of the gospel, through any image. What it asks of us is not arbitrary; God is not giving us hoops to jump through. Of course, if there were a hoop to jump through to gain eternal blessedness and I could do it, I would. (I hope.) But what would that say about God? That he is arbitrary? That he wants us to pay in some way, even though he says his offer is free? I often have non-Christians ask me, "Why doesn't God just save me? Why do I have to believe and promise to obey and trust, and all that?" It does feel arbitrary to them, as if God were saying, "Look, get at least a little bit religious and I'll ease up and let you in." The God and Father of our Lord Jesus Christ is far better than that.

Letting these gospel images paint their pictures for us is a great help here. They help us see how "the work of God" is not a list of arbitrary tasks, things God just made up. Through these concrete pictures we see the logic of what is required of us. We can see how what we are told to do brings us into the story being told, for "the work of God is this: to believe in the one he has sent" (John 6:29). Each of the images uses its terms to talk about the "work" of believing. The tasks they set us to are the definition of being saved. As I quoted from C. S. Lewis earlier, "Repentance . . . is simply a description of what going back to him is like."[3]

Let's look and see how the call of the gospel is simply a description of what it means to come home and accept the welcome of the Father. First, we have to admit we have been foolish, hurtful children: "Father, I have sinned." If you don't think what you are doing is wrong, you are not going to stop. No good parent wants to see a child grovel, but they rejoice when the child realizes self-destructive behavior and turns around.

Then we have to abandon our lives in the far-off country, dropping our schemes for life on our own. This is simply what it means to come home. We leave the other place behind; it is no longer our home. We must leave behind all our strategies of self-provision. And coming home itself is a statement of trust in the Father. To lean on anyone is to take up the risks of trust. We have to believe that the Father can care for us.

And we must be willing to suffer the pains and rejections of the true Son, what all true children of God will suffer in a faithless world. Our great gift, our inheritance, is the ability to be with God and call him Father. Call God Father, though, and the world will treat us like the Son. This is all just reality; real actions have real consequences. And our homecoming in Jesus is very real.

COMING HOME

The Father gives us no arbitrary tasks in order to punish us or make us prove our love. But we do have to come to our senses and come home. Coming home, accepting the gift, can be hard. Responding to the call is hard for different people in different ways.

Julie had to admit that her very nice life was not enough. She was not outwardly starving or stumbling through life. If she stayed where she was, she would be a fine, upstanding, functional member of society. And there would be a great aching emptiness inside. She had to admit that all the good gifts in her life were just signs and pointers, given to her so that she could recognize her Father's greater goodness. If she clung to them, it would be like trying to take his money and go to live elsewhere.

She also had to tell her very nice, supportive, Buddhist parents that she had turned from their religion and embraced a new Father in heaven. That step took a long time, and she did it in fear and trembling. Would they reject her? Would her heavenly Father take care of her if they did? But coming home to the house of the Father means that we can no longer rely on all that used to give us security.

Lee had to take the bitter walk home, admitting he had been a fool. He also had to confess that he had caused others pain as he tried to avoid pain himself. "I have sinned against heaven and against you. I've gotten myself into a bad place, and I need to come home."

He also had to give up his angry shell, his armor of deciding to trust no one. All those habits of self-protection, and the comfort of resentful anger, had to be left behind. But how much sweeter was the welcome he found! When Jesus tells the story of that younger son's return, he does not take time to describe the look on the son's face or his reaction to the welcome of the Father. He hardly needs to. Can't you imagine his relief, wonder and joy? I've seen that face many times. I see it on Lee when he tells his story and says, "And now I know I have a Father in God."

YOU ARE ALWAYS WITH ME . . .

Now that we have the younger son home, it's time to turn to the older, the second lost son. This gospel image is a powerful word, not just for those outside the church. There are many, apparently at home, who need this message.

Meanwhile, the older son was in the field. When he came near the house, he heard music and dancing. So he called one of the servants and asked him what was going on. "Your brother has come," he replied, "and your father has killed the fattened calf because he has him back safe and sound."

The older brother became angry and refused to go in. So his father went out and pleaded with him. But he answered his father, "Look! All these years I've been slaving for you and never disobeyed your orders. Yet you never gave me even a young goat so I could celebrate with my friends. But when this son of yours who has squandered your property with prostitutes comes home, you kill the fattened calf for him!"

"My son," the father said, "you are always with me, and everything I have is yours. But we had to celebrate and be glad, because this brother of yours was dead and is alive again; he was lost and is found." (Luke 15:25-32)

"All these years I've been slaving for you." In the household of such a father, this son toils like a slave. But the reality is a household of compassion and rich provision: "You are always with me, and everything I have is yours." But this son, living in a grim fantasy of oppression and scarcity, says, "You never gave me even a young goat." This son is lost too; he also must come to his senses.

Too many Christians live in that grim unreality where they are ruled by a stingy father. Some are feeling what the older son does; they are living in anger and resentment. They've worked so hard to be right, to do right, so where is their reward? And what is wrong with all those slackers?

Brent, a former student of mine, was always hard on himself as he followed Jesus. He was slaving away to be good enough. It was sometimes hard to watch. He could also be pretty hard on others. That slavery and its resentment have followed him through the years; he has left four different churches in judgment and anger. He's a Christian, a brother I love, who needs the gospel to soak even deeper into his soul. I hold onto hope for Brent because I know how persistent his Father is. God will continue to show him grace until he begins to receive his adoption as a son as freely as it is being given.

DESPERATE CHILDREN

People working for hard bosses are not always living in anger though. Fear and anxiety are also part of a slave's life. These signs of slaving are also among us in the church, and they are signs that we don't know our Father.

Kathy is one of many Christians who struggle with perfectionism. Excellence is good, but a desperate need to have everything right is slavery. When the demand to have every T crossed seems to come from an omnipotent and all-seeing God, it can be a crushing weight. With her own father leaving her family when she was young, is she trying in some broken way to win his love again? She's not sure; the feelings are tangled deep in her heart and past. She only knows she feels the compulsion to be good enough.

But she is also coming to know the sweet sanity of being a true child of the good Father. Hearing the gospel as adoption is the medicine she needs. She has spent a good amount of time dwelling on that gospel truth, sitting still in the knowledge of her Father's embrace, knowing that her Father is standing by her with open arms—right now. And there is freedom with him that makes her able to say, "So I don't have time to make homemade brownies for the meeting. Sometimes it will just have to be Oreos." And she smiles the smile of a secure and beloved daughter. It's one more sign that the gospel of adoption is gaining ground in her soul, day by day.

. . . AND ALL I HAVE IS YOURS

Alicia had another struggle. She was feeling the years go by, and she was still single. Was loneliness going to be a chronic fact of her life? Instead of playing the world's dating game, she had focused on serving God. She had been good! Yet he hadn't given her a companion. Or even promised one. Was he going to be good to her?

The Son knew how to lean on his Father, and he taught Alicia how. Once, as she shared this struggle with me, she said, "I hate this. It hurts! . . . But I know my Father will take care of me," and her tear-filled eyes were deep wells of belief. They spoke to me, again, the good news of how the Father has embraced us in Jesus, how he will give us everything we need and will carry us all the way home.

When I was a child, my dad—I don't call him my "adoptive father," he's my dad—would tuck me in every night by saying the twenty-third psalm with me. The first image in that well-worn psalm is the Lord protecting and providing like a shepherd. But then David's image of the Lord becomes a host at a feast, lavishly providing for him, honoring and protecting him—not unlike what the prodigal son's father did for him. David's conclusion is etched in my mind, as I fell asleep on thousands of nights hearing Dad say, "Surely goodness and love will follow me all the days of my life, and I will dwell in the house of the Lord forever." Those are the words of a secure child and, because of Jesus, they can be anyone's. They can be yours—even tonight.

KINGDOM

A Good World Order

I was sitting with my neighbor having a quiet cup of coffee. The sunshine of a pleasant day streamed in the windows as we talked of . . . racism and brutality. An African American author, he had just written a book on racial profiling and acts of police brutality. I read his book and invited him over because I wanted to get to know him, to see what he cared about. What he cared about was the society in which his children were growing up and that it was not a safe place for them. He said he hadn't wanted to write that book because "all I really want is to be able to live my life." But after the latest incident—another innocent black man killed, the police officer who shot him acquitted—he couldn't keep silent. I longed for the gospel to speak to him. I felt that I, too, could not keep silent.

Later I was at the wedding of a relative who has found peace and meaning through Buddhism. It was a beautiful service. Over the weekend, his story came out in various conversations. He hadn't been satisfied with the answers and the faith he had been given, but he loved life and kept asking questions. Once, during a hiking trip, he stumbled on a Buddhist retreat center and was won over by its peace, gentleness and respect for life. He and his friends were captivated by a vision not only of inner peace but also of harmony with all life. Talking with them, I longed not only to affirm their vision but also to show them its fulfillment in Jesus.

So many people are looking for a better world, and the gospel has a word for them. They feel life's brokenness and unfulfilled promise on so many levels. Our souls, our society, our planet are not what they should be—and we feel it. The gospel speaks to this pain and to the dream of better things. It proclaims the coming of a new world, a whole world filled with whole people. It does this in the clearest and strongest way through the image of the kingdom of God. The kingdom is the new world order brought by the true king, Jesus.

THE BIG PICTURE

We looked at the gospel pictured as new life, and it was powerful. It showed how deeply necessary and renewing God's gift is. But it can be a little vague. The image of adoption sharpened the focus and showed us the character of the life we have been given—a welcome into the love of the Father to share what he has always given his Son. But the family image alone might leave us with a small and cozy picture of God's work. The life, death and resurrection of Jesus does bring us close to God, but it also changes the whole universe and reorders all of human life. The kingdom of God has come; this is no mere private salvation.

We have a tendency to think of the gospel, and all religion really, as a matter of personal morality. A friend who wasn't a Christian caught me in this. I once took Yoshi, a Japanese grad student in economics, to hear a talk on campus by a local pastor. Yoshi wasn't then a Christian. We met in our apartment building, became friends and began to investigate the Bible together. I was excited that night for Yoshi to hear a clear presentation of the gospel.

But the pastor surprised me, and spoke on the Ten Commandments instead. Walking home, I apologized to Yoshi for the talk not being what I had expected, an exposé of private sin and a call to personal relationship with God. "Oh no!" he said, "it was very interesting. Every society needs a firm basis for economics and conduct. I'm very impressed Christianity gives such a strong foundation."

A vision for all of life, salvation for the whole world—this is what the gospel brings. The foundations were laid in the Old Testament. Jesus is the cornerstone, and the apostles carried the message of this kingdom out into the world. Paul paints the good news very simply in kingdom terms: God "has rescued us from the dominion of darkness and brought us into the kingdom of the Son he loves" (Colossians 1:13).

The dominion of darkness was over us. There is a fundamental evil in the world, a crushing disorder that we feel in many ways. My neighbor felt it as he considered the plight of his people. My Buddhist friends feel it as a disharmony of life in the world. God long ago promised his people that the dominion of darkness would end and that he would make the world the good place it was always meant to be. And the people of Israel long held onto that hope.

A VISION OF HOPE

In Isaiah we see this promise, this word of hope. To a people often oppressed by outside powers and by their own corrupt rulers, the knowledge that God would act in this world was a great comfort. In Isaiah we hear that God will send a ruler to set things right:

> The Spirit of the LORD will rest on him—
> > the Spirit of wisdom and of understanding,
> > the Spirit of counsel and of power,
> > the Spirit of knowledge and of the fear of the LORD—
> and he will delight in the fear of the LORD.
> > He will not judge by what he sees with his eyes,
> > or decide by what he hears with his ears;
> but with righteousness he will judge the needy,
> > with justice he will give decisions for the poor of the earth.
> > He will strike the earth with the rod of his mouth;
> > with the breath of his lips he will slay the wicked.
> Righteousness will be his belt
> > and faithfulness the sash around his waist. (Isaiah 11:2-5)

A person of authority and power who actually cares for his people and is full of wisdom—what a relief! And what would the world then be like when it is run this way? Here the prophet becomes very symbolic as he shows the world at peace, old enemies living together and no reason for the weak to ever be afraid:

> The wolf will live with the lamb,
>> the leopard will lie down with the goat,
>> the calf and the lion and the yearling together;
>> and a little child will lead them.
> The cow will feed with the bear,
>> their young will lie down together,
>> and the lion will eat straw like the ox.
> The infant will play near the hole of the cobra,
>> and the young child put his hand into the viper's nest.
> They will neither harm nor destroy
>> on all my holy mountain,
>> for the earth will be full of the knowledge of the LORD
>> as the waters cover the sea. (Isaiah 11:6-9)

This was the hope of Israel, and while it was almost too good to be true, while it was hard to imagine what it would even look like, many clung to that hope in their hearts. Like my neighbor who sees the dominion of racism crushing those he loves, yet still hopes for America to live up to its ideals, or my Buddhist friends who actively seek for peace in this broken world—they could not let go of the dream.

THE ARRIVAL

Jesus steps into this brokenness, and this longing. He steps into view ready to start making this kingdom real from the very beginning. His first public words in Luke proclaim that the kingdom has come. He reminds the people of the old dream with another ancient prophesy of Isaiah that speaks of the coming King and his kingdom of peace. And then he gives them some news.

> He went to Nazareth, where he had been brought up, and on the Sabbath day he went into the synagogue, as was his custom. And

he stood up to read. The scroll of the prophet Isaiah was handed
to him. Unrolling it, he found the place where it is written:

"The Spirit of the Lord is on me,
　　because he has anointed me
　　to preach good news to the poor.
He has sent me to proclaim freedom for the prisoners
　　and recovery of sight for the blind,
to release the oppressed,
　　to proclaim the year of the Lord's favor."

Then he rolled up the scroll, gave it back to the attendant and
sat down. The eyes of everyone in the synagogue were fastened on
him, and he began by saying to them, "Today this scripture is fulfilled in your hearing." (Luke 4:16-21)

"Today this scripture is fulfilled." These were words of authority.
Anointing from God meant authority and power; his hearers would
know that. But authority for what? For changing the fortunes of the
poor, giving freedom to the imprisoned and oppressed, restoring sight
to the blind. This was not a sermon; it was an announcement of a new
order. It was a notification of a whole new epoch: the year of the Lord's
favor. Jesus had not come to talk about God's new order; he had come to
bring it.

THE HEALING TOUCH

And he sets out to do just that. His every word and action made that
kingdom real and showed what it is like. Looking at just one act from
his life paints a beautiful picture of this new kingdom.

In Luke 7 we see him walking into a town, just as a funeral is coming
out. He sees he is coming to a people in mourning. The dead man was
"the only son of his mother, and she was a widow." While this may be
hard in our society, it was so much more so in theirs. This woman was
now alone, with no provider, no protector in the world. But a good king
is a protector and provider: "When the Lord saw her, his heart went out

to her and he said, 'Don't cry.' Then he went up and touched the coffin, and those carrying it stood still. He said, 'Young man, I say to you, get up!' The dead man sat up and began to talk, and Jesus gave him back to his mother" (Luke 7:13-15).

The people standing there did not say, "How amazing, a miracle!" or "How wonderful for her!" They said, "God has come to help his people." They saw a shattered life restored, the vulnerable given shelter and power that restores life. And they knew what it meant: the King has come with compassion to look after his people and make them whole.

Jesus brought the kingdom with him wherever he walked, even into the halls of the powers-that-be. When he went up to the temple at Jerusalem, he knew what he would find there—he had been there before. But now it was time to loose the chains there. The famous scene of Jesus driving the moneychangers from the temple is not just a scene of passionate religious devotion; it is one of holy justice. He cleared out a "den of robbers," kicking out a corrupt alliance of business interests and religious-political leaders. And he restored the outer courts of the temple to the religious have-nots, the Gentiles, so the temple could once again be "a house of prayer for all nations." He put himself on the line to clean up the system for his people.[1]

WHOLENESS FOR ALL OUR BROKENNESS

When I see how Jesus brought the kingdom to us, I think of one of his modern followers. Sometimes the accounts of the Bible seem unreal, caught in stained glass. Hearing the story of a modern follower of Jesus helps me get a feel for a life that carries the kingdom of God's wholeness wherever it goes. David Livingstone was an explorer and missionary to Africa when most Europeans were concerned with building their own kingdoms—on the backs of others, if they had to. But he came to that place with a word of truth—and true care to back it up. He brought his medical skills to serve and heal. And, just as Jesus' zeal for God moved him to clear the temple, Livingstone's moved him to fight against the slave trade.

One short biography I came across said, "Livingstone was a curious combination of missionary, doctor, explorer, scientist and anti-slavery activist."[2] A curious combination, unless you understand a heart that wants to move out and touch the world around it, finding all its potential and healing all its brokenness.

Jesus was the one sent to do this, empowered to change the whole world with his life. His mission was not just to end up with one life well lived but to initiate a kingdom that transformed the whole world. He said the kingdom of God is "like a mustard seed, which is the smallest seed you plant in the ground. Yet when planted, it grows and becomes the largest of all garden plants, with such big branches that the birds of the air can perch in its shade" (Mark 4:31-32). He saw the kingdom beginning with just one life and then spreading out to cover the whole earth.

ENTERING THE KINGDOM

But what has happened? Where is this kingdom? For a worldwide revolution, the kingdom of God can be pretty hard to spot. Where is all the peace and wholeness? Where is the cataclysmic reverse, the longed-for defeat of evil? Theologians sum it up by saying that kingdom is "already, but not yet."

Jesus clearly thought of the kingdom as "already," as starting now. In the first chapter of Mark, he begins by preaching, "The time has come. The kingdom of God is near. Repent and believe the good news!" (Even the word for good news—*euangelion*—is a kingdom word. It is the proclamation of a new Caesar's reign. And, with Jesus, the new reign had come.) The kingdom is active here and now: "If I drive out demons by the Spirit of God, then the kingdom of God has come upon you" (Matthew 12:28). The king has landed in occupied territory. The change has begun; the kingdom has come.

But not completely. The kingdom is here, but we must stop resisting and actively enter it. As Jesus said, "Woe to you, teachers of the law and Pharisees, you hypocrites! You shut the kingdom of heaven in men's faces.

You yourselves do not enter, nor will you let those enter who are trying to" (Matthew 23:13), and "I tell you the truth, the tax collectors and the prostitutes are entering the kingdom of God ahead of you" (21:31).

"Enter the kingdom" or "inherit the kingdom" are how this image says, "Get saved." But entering the kingdom now is not the whole story. We still look forward; we wait for the full coming of the kingdom. All true subjects of the king cry out, "Your kingdom come, your will be done on earth as it is in heaven" (6:10), and they won't be satisfied—or at home here, until the kingdom has fully come.

LIVING ON THE CUSP

History is the tale of kingdoms coming and going, and the Bible invites us to picture a coming kingdom, so let's look at a story from history to help us picture life under a coming kingdom.

Edward Plantagenet was an English king laying claim to Scotland. (This is the king who provoked William "Braveheart" Wallace to rebel. Edward was not a nice man, but for our picture here, he'll do.) He came with his army and his nobles to the border of Scotland and camped there, flags flying. He then sent heralds into Scotland, calling its nobles to come do homage and pay fealty to him. If they did, they would "enter the king's peace." They would come under his rule and his protection— and they would march with him when he marched. If they didn't—well, either you came to Edward or he came for you.

King Jesus has come to our borders. He's made his presence known, but he hasn't yet come in power to press his claims. He has called us to join him, and his messengers are moving in the world. They come with an announcement that requires decision. It is a call to enter the King's peace. God will not allow his beloved world to lie in ruins forever. He has come to remove all evil from the world. He will act soon. But, for now, the call is still going out.

A KINGDOM ON THE MOVE

Ever since Jesus sent them out, his followers have been living in this new kingdom and moving out in his Spirit. Luke shows the earliest groups of believers living under this new order:

> All the believers were one in heart and mind. No one claimed that any of his possessions was his own, but they shared everything they had. With great power the apostles continued to testify to the resurrection of the Lord Jesus, and much grace was upon them all. There were no needy persons among them. For from time to time those who owned lands or houses sold them, brought the money from the sales and put it at the apostles' feet, and it was distributed to anyone as he had need. (Acts 4:32-35)

This community that lived under the vision of God's peace and provision moved out into the Roman Empire and brought the kingdom with them. They called out to God for the good of their nation, and they gave what they could spare for the healing and comfort of those around them. Defending Christianity around A.D. 200, Tertullian said that when Christians assembled, "We pray, too, for the emperors, for their ministers and for all in authority, for the welfare of the world, for the prevalence of peace." And when they got together, money changed hands, but it was for the good of others: "These gifts are, as it were, piety's deposit fund. For they are not taken thence and spent on feasts, and drinking-bouts, and eating-houses, but to support and bury poor people, to supply the wants of boys and girls destitute of means and parents, and of old persons confined now to the house; such, too, as have suffered shipwreck."[3] This is just what the followers of Jesus do, day in and day out: pray and work for the healing and wholeness of their nation and its people.

And they work to bring wholeness across racial and cultural lines scarred by a history of fear and hatred. Around A.D. 400, St. Patrick, a Romanized Briton, was captured as a teen by an Irish slave-raiding party and taken to Ireland. After years of captivity, he was able to escape. But he later obeyed the call of God to go back and serve the Irish people. He spent the rest of his life for a people who had enslaved him, bringing it the light of the gospel and the wholeness of life that comes with it.

There are so many stories, told and untold, of the kingdom weaving its influence through history, as Jesus said, like yeast working through dough (see Matthew 13:33). William Wilberforce was a parliamentarian who led Great Britain to abolish the slave trade.[4] It took his life's energy and entire career, and he only heard that he had won on his deathbed. Yet he won, and now he has a place in history. And Candace, whom few have heard of, is likewise spending her life for the kingdom. As she shows me pictures of women she is helping leave lives of prostitution, I know that her story will also be a bright spot in the kingdom's history.

Jesus has set all this in motion. The character of the kingdom is set by the character of the king, the one who came to give his life for his people. To get to the bottom of this kingdom, to find out what it is all about and to enter in, we have to come back to the king and watch him live and die for us.

THE HEART OF KINGSHIP

Jesus came with a kingdom wholly different from any the world had yet seen. He comes to us very differently than an Edward Plantagenet, even while in some ways his kingship is the same. (Or perhaps we should say that Edward in some ways acted like the true King and in other ways he failed.) Napoleon is widely quoted as saying, "Alexander, Caesar, Charlemagne, and myself have all founded great empires. Upon what did we rest the creations of our genius? Upon force. Jesus Christ founded an empire on love, and this day millions would die for him."

The foundations of this empire are radically different from anything we have ever seen. Here we come down to the heart, the core of this new order, and we see a person who would die for us.

> Jesus called them together and said, "You know that those who are
> regarded as rulers of the Gentiles lord it over them, and their high
> officials exercise authority over them. Not so with you. Instead,
> whoever wants to become great among you must be your servant,

and whoever wants to be first must be slave of all. For even the Son of Man did not come to be served, but to serve, and to give his life as a ransom for many." (Mark 10:42-45)

Jesus not only shows his greatness by dying for us, he also becomes first by dying for all. The hymn preserved in Philippians 2 shows us the path to the victory of the king: he is exalted because he gave his life to his people.

And being found in appearance as a man, he humbled himself and became obedient to death—even death on a cross! Therefore God exalted him to the highest place and gave him the name that is above every name, that at the name of Jesus every knee should bow, in heaven and on earth and under the earth, and every tongue confess that Jesus Christ is Lord, to the glory of God the Father. (Philippians 2:8-11)

Though he had the rights of the Creator, he laid them down. He then earned a kingship over creation by becoming one with it and laying down his life for it. What Pilate said in irony, "Here is your king" (John 19:14), was the absolute truth. Here, innocent, but broken for you, is your king. Jesus had told Pilate, "My kingdom is not of this world" (John 18:36). It was not a matter of geography, but of kind. His was a kingship that ruled by giving and where the greatest gave the most to all. His gift of his own life, his suffering and death, was his victory. His crucifixion was his ascension to the throne and the exercise of his kingship. The cross did not veil his royal glory; it revealed it. Calvary is his throne. For all time we will live under the rule of the Lamb, who stands at the center of the throne, "looking as if it had been slain" (Revelation 5:6).

It won't be long before every knee shall bow, not because a strong hand presses them down, but because the truth of the matter is clear: the One who has loved us with his life is our rightful Lord.

A BEAUTIFUL DEMAND

Bowing to someone else. Here comes the demanding beauty of this image. We have to admit that not only does the earth need a better rule but so do we. To "confess that Jesus Christ is Lord" means that we agree that the word of Jesus should be law to us; the character that shapes his kingdom should also shape our lives. He is our better, and we must let him lead us.

The image of the kingdom shows us repentance as a change of personal allegiance. "Joy to the world, the Lord is come! / Let Earth receive her King!" We must all acknowledge him, as the psalmist says, "Therefore, you kings, be wise; / be warned, you rulers of the earth. / Serve the LORD with fear and rejoice with trembling. / Kiss the Son, lest he be angry / and you be destroyed in your way, for his wrath can flare up in a moment. / Blessed are all who take refuge in him" (Psalm 2:10-12).

This is no exercise in mental assent, no acceptance of abstract principles. It is about *him*. Will you love him or oppose him? He brings a reign of love and peace, and his love for the world moves him to rid it of evil, oppression and injustice. When he moves, will you be for him or against him?

Other ways of speaking the gospel might seem to leave a loophole for conversion without action. They are easier to twist into "receive the gift, and relax." This kingdom image can help us bring love and obedience together: "Whoever has my commands and obeys them, he is the one who loves me" (John 14:21). Seeing Jesus as my king makes it clear that love and obedience are one step. How could you love your king and not obey him? A true king says "I love you" by saying, "I will lead you and provide for you, no matter what it costs me, to the very end." And the loyal friend, the beloved and loving subject, says "I love you" with "And I will follow you, no matter the cost, to the very end." Dealing with your Lord, obedience is trust is love.

Of course, in this world, leaders often don't act like the true King. Then it is not only unsafe to totally obey them, it is unloving. Wayward leaders can be served when their subjects correct or even defy them, hoping they return to the true path of leadership. But Jesus is always true, and it is always safe to obey.

When my friend Yoshi finally bowed his head to pray and "accept

Jesus," he was accepting a new ruler. He was admitting his need to live in a whole new way, to fit into that "impressive foundation" that God has laid for the world. He was saying he would love his new Lord and follow in his way.

GOOD NEWS FOR WHOM?

God has shown the power of the gospel in the coming of a kingdom that pushes back the dominion of darkness. And this has been good news to many. The king has come to inaugurate a brand new day and to give a call to allegiance. How can we see the kingdom break in, even today? How can this archaic language help us witness today? Who has ears to hear this good news?

WHEN DEMOCRACIES DAYDREAM

When missionaries go to tribal peoples, they often find surprising beliefs beneath the surface. Under the polytheistic, animistic, everyday religion and thought, there are old stories and distant memories. They will tell of long ago, when the people had been in touch with the one Creator. But the stories also explain how, now, the people are subject to all the smaller and darker powers.[5] A good missionary will find those memories of the true God in a culture and show how Jesus meets and fulfills them.

Coming to the modern West, what would a sensitive missionary see? All our workaday world is ruled by market forces, corporate powers and public opinions. But beneath that is a persistent dream of the good kingdom. Millions of adults spend hours upon hours reading stories of loyalty, service and sacrifice, of heroes and heroines and the return to the throne of a true princess or prince. That this goes beyond a tiny market or obscure genre hardly needs to be said, especially in the wake of the Lord of the Rings films. But what are we so thirsty for? Are all those readers, moviegoers and historic re-enactors longing for a glorious past or for something that hasn't yet come?

At my college there was a group of students who played fantasy games and staged mock medieval battles. They were part of the Society for Creative Anachronisms. Now *there* is a cultural renewal idea: a community that brings to life things that don't seem to belong in this time. What if Christians were creative about reviving ideas of loyalty and allegiance, true nobility and the fight of good against evil?

Can we do this and not become angry, combative and triumphalistic? Of course, if we stay in step with the character of our King, the servant of all. Apart from him, any effort will become twisted. That's why loyalty to him is the key.

Wouldn't this be a telling of the good news that would speak to the undercurrents of our age? Couldn't this be hope to a part of our souls that is starving in our mechanistic world? We need to develop the skill of telling the gospel as the tale of the coming of the one true King.

UNDER PRESSURE

The idea of the kingdom gave me good news to tell my neighbor, the author. If the gospel I knew was only about private sin and salvation, I would not see one of his key needs: to be freed from the oppression of racism. The gospel of the kingdom had helped me to see the big picture that he did. It also gave me something to offer him. He could not be silent about what was happening to his people—and I could say God was not silent either.

I told him of college students who—in service of King Jesus—served in the city and overseas, learning how the kingdom could come with good news for the poor. I had seen so many pray like those believers in Acts and seen them given power to speak truth and do acts of healing and mercy. I could tell of graduates who started strategic businesses, who taught in the city, who did social work—who prayed with their lives "your kingdom come." As he offered me his insights and feelings, I could offer him a gospel big enough to face the evil he saw in his world.

KINGDOM HOPE

Christians also need a gospel this big. Maria was a college Christian overwhelmed. She knew God loved the world, but it was all so broken. The more she learned, the more oppression and pain she saw. "The dominion of darkness" is not just a poetic phrase, and she was coming to feel it. Unlike many of us, she was unable to ignore the reality of the world's darkness. It brought her to the edge of depression.

Then she read a short book that told of a gospel that reached into darkness and of a kingdom people devoted to a servant king. It was the story of the founding of the International Justice Mission, a group devoted to helping those caught in wage slavery, prostitution rings and extortion by corrupt officials.[6] With stories of Christians living their lives so others could be free, and a real-life call to action that Maria could respond to, it was a doorway to hope. It gave her tangible evidence that God's goodness was strong enough and big enough to really deal with evil. The gospel was good news for all that she had so recently seen—not good news just for her soul but also for the whole world.

If we live in this world with our eyes open, the gospel of the coming kingdom is hope beyond hope.

Outposts

A maintenance man walked into a meeting and found himself in an outpost of that coming kingdom. He had passed back and forth as he did his work in the convent, and he saw my wife and her teammates working and talking—and he was drawn to them. They were men and women, Asian and black and white and Latino, working together as a community—and loving it. They weren't skirting issues of ethnicity and racism either. Often we settle for that cheap and temporary peace. Instead they were working on what it meant for their ministry to reflect the reign of Jesus over all peoples.

So, one evening as they were watching and discussing a Spike Lee film, Frank came in and joined them. He was welcomed in, and he began to tell his own story. I don't know if he heard the word *kingdom* that evening, but I know he was with people who knew it and had it in their bloodstream. As an African American man, he hadn't seen much reason for hope for real community across ethnic and racial lines. But there he found it. It was a safe place, and he came in from the cold to enjoy the warmth of the kingdom for a while.

This group knew the gospel brings a new order to all our relationships. They knew Jesus restores both souls and communities of souls, so they were able to fully inherit a kingdom of light that could shine out to a passer-by and call him in.

History has often seen cities full of cheering people, waving and dancing as a liberating army rolls into town. So many waiting so long for freedom to come. But the euphoria soon fades. The new regime is not all goodness and light. All hopes disappoint—almost. There is one liberation that will bring an unending celebration, one new order that will be even more than it promised.

And we get to sneak into town in advance of the main column, to spread the news and get the people ready. The kingdom is coming. The kingdom is here. That is good enough news to get us celebrating, even now.

part two
IMAGES OF MERCY AND RESTORATION

Here we come to our second set of images. We have seen some pictures of the gospel that focus on what we were *saved for*, images of the life we are moving toward. Before God gets us all the way there, however, there are some realities he has to deal with, things we need to be *saved from*. There is evil and brokenness in us and in the world, and it must be dealt with before all will be well with us.

The following images are at their best when they tell us this part of the story. Again, like any telling of the gospel, these images tell the whole story: what we needed to be saved from, what God did in Jesus, and the new life we are brought into. But these next images seem to make the most sense in light of what we need to be saved *from*, the evil we are leaving behind.

Here, in these images of mercy and restoration, we are looking at how we need to be saved from ourselves. Part of the problem is us, what we have done. Later on, in part three, we'll look at how Jesus saves us from outside forces and the evil of others. For we need to be saved both from the wrongs we have done and the wrongs done to us. But what we'll see first are three images of how he deals with the wrong we ourselves have done. For, as one confession says, "We have left undone those things which we ought to have done; and we have done those things which we ought not to have done; and there is no health in us."[1] But this is not enough to stop God.

JUSTIFICATION

Being Right with God

Outwardly two people may seem as different as could be, yet might be facing the same problem and need to hear the same word from God.

Tony sat at the bar with his new friend, Jason. They were having a beer together, and Jason was telling him how cool God is. It sounded good; it really did. But Tony knew he wasn't God's type. He had joked with Jason about the drinking and the sex, but there were some women he had really hurt. Now that he thought about it, he just couldn't see himself ever living that down. He couldn't get from where he was to where this happy Christian guy was.

Angie was a good church girl, getting baptized at just the right age, and everyone was pleased and proud. But as she looked back out at the crowd, in a moment of clarity, she said to herself, *I can't believe I'm standing here, lying to all these people.* She looked like she was in, she talked like she was in, everyone thought she was in—but she knew she wasn't that good. She was a fake, and the guilt of her lie weighed on her.

Our sin has themes, recurrent patterns of damage done to us and our relationship with God. Both Tony and Angie saw themselves and saw God's people and knew they didn't belong. And they were right. But grace also has themes, and its music is much more powerful. The language of justification paints an image that shows the way for these two people—and many others—to find peace. Through it, we can hear God say, "Don't worry, and don't pretend. Just trust. You're okay with me. Now, let's get on with life." The good news is just that, and the language of justification brings this aspect of the cross out in plain view.

GOD HOLDS COURT

The vocabulary of justification brings us images from the legal world and the law court. What we must do first, then, is pull up our image of that court. Let yourself into that familiar scene; picture the defendant and the prosecution, the witnesses and jury, and the lofty judge on the bench. The law rules, and appeals to it are made as evidence and arguments go back and forth—until the gavel falls and the verdict is given. Got the picture? Good. Now let it go.

The great court of God in the Bible has some similarities to our modern Western court, but it is also very different. Paul, rooted in the Old Testament, has in mind the great court held at the end of time, when all the nations will be judged.[1] The image here is the court of an ancient Near Eastern king. There are no checks and balances in this court; there is no power or authority behind or above the king. In himself he has the wisdom and the power, the authority to pronounce judgment and the ability to carry it through. He weighs the evidence and gives his judgment. As he says, so it is.

GETTING PERSONAL

In this way the great court is more like being hauled up before your parents than being tried in a modern court. It is very immediate and personal. You come eye to eye with one who knows you and will decide what is to be done with you.

We must always think of God's law as a very personal affair. The law in the Old Testament was part of the covenant relationship between God and his people. It was based on God's character and described the kind of character his people should have and how they should relate to him. To break the law was to violate that relationship. This is how James sees it: "For whoever keeps the whole law and yet stumbles at just one point is guilty of breaking all of it. For he who said, 'Do not commit adultery,' also said, 'Do not murder.' If you do not commit adultery but do commit murder, you have become a lawbreaker" (James 2:10-11).

"For he who said." The relationship to the Lawgiver is the key thing. So, to be declared a righteous person in that great court isn't so much a declaration that you have done a, b and c, and haven't done x, y and z—the question is, are you right with God? The righteous do obey and don't sin, but they act this way because they are being faithful to the covenant relationship. Faithful to the law of that covenant, they stand in the circle of his approval. They are his.

PERSONAL AND PUBLIC

While God's great court is personal, it is not a private chat. The scene is very weighty and very public. Israel was given visions, like those in the book of Joel, of all the nations being judged on that day. All peoples would stand and face God and hear his decision about them. They saw that court as the time when God would judge the Gentile nations for the oppressive, violent, ungodly people they were. Of course, Israel would be shown as God's approved people, his faithful ones who were right to wait for him, even when things looked grim. They would stand in the circle of his approval.

But some prophets also made it clear that Israel did not always live up to the name God had given them. Those prophets, such as Amos, made it clear that even Israel would be judged—for being the oppressive, violent, ungodly people *they* were. That prophetic vision of the great court was given to shatter a proud people's false confidence. It raised the question "Who is the true Israel?" Who are the people who really follow God, the people with whom he will be pleased when he comes to judge? Who would stand in the place of his favor?

Plenty of people wanted to say, "That's us." Reading these prophecies in Scripture, this or that sect has always been claiming they are the faithful remnant. They are the ones who have done what God really wanted, acted in a way that honors him. They are the ones who will be declared right when "he will judge the world in righteousness and the peoples in his truth" (Psalm 96:13). Down through the centuries, then, it was an open question: Who will be justified in the end? All most people could do was try their best and live in hope. And then came Jesus.

UNDER JUDGMENT

Paul takes up this picture of the great court of God and uses it to frame Jesus for us. As a Jewish teacher, Paul knew the picture of the great court very well. Like many zealous Jews, he was sure it would be a great day for him and people like him. Coming to know his Messiah, however, helped him see that ancient vision in a new light. We'll skip an interpretive stone across the opening chapters of Romans to watch him paint his picture of the gospel as justification.

Paul begins by showing how we stand without Jesus, and the picture is grim. Even as we start, there is a dark, lowering cloud over our race: "The wrath of God is being revealed from heaven against all the godlessness and wickedness of human beings who suppress the truth by their wickedness" (Romans 1:18 TNIV). The righteous Judge is watching and active now, even though our "court date" is in the future: "Because of your stubbornness and your unrepentant heart, you are storing up wrath against yourself for the day of God's wrath, when his righteous judgment will be revealed" (Romans 2:5). While that terrible day is still in the future, we can look forward and anticipate the verdict. Israel often did this and anticipated the verdict on other nations; Paul looks and sees an open-and-shut case against *all* people:

> What shall we conclude then? Are we any better? Not at all! We have already made the charge that Jews and Gentiles alike are all under sin. As it is written: "There is no one righteous, not even one; there is no one who understands, no one who seeks God. All have turned away, they have together become worthless; there is no one who does good, not even one. . . . "
>
> Now we know that whatever the law says, it says to those who are under the law, so that every mouth may be silenced and the whole world held accountable to God. Therefore no one will be declared righteous in his sight by observing the law; rather, through the law we become conscious of sin. (Romans 3:9-12, 19-20)

Every mouth silenced before the truth. Our constant testimony in our own defense will be stilled. That silence will be profound—and very uncomfortable. Rationalizations that we have always hidden behind will fall away, and we will stand exposed. And few of us realize just how naked we will feel: we often fail to notice the steady stream of our own "testimony" about ourselves, our constant efforts at self-justification. We fail to notice it because we hear it all the time. How many times have I sat in a coffee shop and overheard "testimonies" like these:

> And then he said to me that he would have gotten the report done on time if he had gotten the data. As if I hadn't been trying to call him all weekend. Then he says that our whole section will have to start working overtime, and he's looking at *me*. Can you believe it? But *you* know, and so does he, that we have been pulling overtime all week. . . ."
>
> "All I said was that *somebody* should clean this up, and then he went ballistic on me."
>
> "If you only knew what I'm dealing with here. . . ."
>
> "I know *that*, but what I was trying to do was . . ."
>
> "Sorry, but the kids needed something just as I was going out the door and the traffic was a little thick. . . . "
>
> "Sorry, but . . . "

I am no different. I once took a challenge to listen to myself for a day. That was twenty years ago, and I still remember what I heard. At home, out with my friends, at the fast-food place where I worked, it all sounded the same. So many of my words were in my own defense: "I knew *that*. . . . Well, I was just about to say . . . I was going to get around to that soon. . . . What I *meant* was this." Beyond my words, I wonder how many of my actions are done to justify my existence, to state my okayness to anyone who might wonder? My clothing, my career moves, the stories I tell . . . how much of what I do is a frantic attempt to show that I am all right? Self-justification is a full-time job.

And listen to us in groups. Our slogans, political speeches, anthems—don't they all proclaim how right we are? And the chatter, the murmur, the dull roar of our constant self-justification rises up before the throne, until God makes the truth clear. He has the law show us who we really are "so that every mouth may be silenced and the whole world held accountable." When the truth has been revealed, what is left to say? Then all the nations will stand in silence, endure his gaze, know the truth—and know they are known.

Tony knew this judgment as he sat in a bar. Angie felt it as she stood in the church. Anyone who lets God's righteous words get through to them will know it. They'll know that the ways they make themselves look and feel okay may work for some audiences, but not for the One who really counts.

We had been wondering who would be able to stand tall on that great day, who would be approved as God's kind of people. And now we know the answer: no one. God has marked out a circle of approval with his law, where anyone who lives his way can stand and find his favor. But the circle is empty. When all the pretense is brushed aside, there is no one who is simply, honestly and wholly good. Humanity has had millennia to try—generation after generation, civilization after civilization—and we have not produced the only thing that matters: good people, people who can look Goodness himself in the eye, unashamed.

HAULED INTO COURT

That is the image Paul paints, of all humanity brought before God and having to face him with nothing they can really say for themselves. I can still remember when I first walked into that image, though at the time I had no idea I would end up there.

At seventeen, I had gotten into a fix. All summer long my cousin Brent and I had been larking about and engaging in, shall we say, "recreational" drug use. Then one Friday, he just disappeared. His parents and mine were frantic, and few people can be as stern as a worried parent. They cornered me in the living room that night and confronted me about our drug use, painting dire scenarios of Brent having run afoul of drug dealers somewhere. I felt like the dregs of humanity. Then I was left alone to ponder my wrongdoing and to fear for my cousin.

Now, if you had a video of what went on in that living room late that night, all you would see would be me sitting, standing or pacing around for a few hours. But in reality, I had entered places best pictured by that great law court. Though I didn't know it when I started, I was going to meet the Judge.

I had thought that I could go to God and ask him a favor. But when I got to the courts of the King, I found that it was time for judgment—and I was on trial. There was a place in that court where a person could stand and talk with God and have their requests considered, but I could not stand there. I had walked in with a life lived against his will, and I was not standing in the circle of his approval.

Please understand. I don't think God wants us to grovel in front of him. And he doesn't meet every seeker's prayer by first throwing their wrongs in their face. I myself had had some warm experiences with God throughout my childhood. His mercy covers us even before we know it. But for me to take my next steps with him, he had to take me to court. He wanted to clear the way for more than occasional brushes with him: he wanted to open up a whole life with him. So, it was my court date, my time to deal with the facts of my life.

So those facts came out. I felt his gaze, the whole place seemed full of his presence, but he was saying nothing. He was just regarding me. As I stood there, I began to see my actions the way he did, and it wasn't pretty. The lies, the hiding and sneaking, the petty disobedience—it all seemed so small and ugly, and obviously wrong. I tried to bargain my way into his favor, but this Judge did not make deals. And the truth was getting clearer by the minute. That terrible silence descended. There was nothing I could say, so I gave up. I told him he was right, my life wasn't good, and from now on I would do it his way.

But the strangest thing happened. I had just pleaded guilty—I had just said I wasn't all right, but then I suddenly felt all right. The weight of the silence lifted, and I felt that the one who was the stern Judge was now smiling at me. That was great, but what happened?

RIGHTEOUSNESS PROVIDED

The words of Scripture help us frame our life and experiences with God, and the court picture helped me look back later and understand what happened. How could I have been so stuck in front of God, so caught by the truth of who I was, and then find myself free to go out and live like one of God's people? How was I made an upstanding citizen of the kingdom, someone God smiles on?

As Paul paints his image of God's great court, he makes the answer clear. We all were standing under judgment in that great silence—I was, Tony was, Angie was and so was every person ever born. But that great King holding court is more than just a judge; he is also a faithful provider, and he provides even the righteousness his people need.

In the midst of that awful silence, God brings forth his provision of righteousness, Jesus. "But now a righteousness from God, apart from law, has been made known, to which the Law and the Prophets testify. This righteousness from God comes through faith in Jesus Christ to all who believe" (Romans 3:21-22). This Righteous One can work for us, his goodness can speak on our behalf: "If anybody does sin, we have one who speaks to the Father in our defense—Jesus Christ, the Righteous One" (1 John 2:1). He came to join us under judgment so he could bring us into the circle of God's approval: "He was delivered over to death for our sins and was raised to life for our justification" (Romans 4:25).

I had given up making my own case and, as the stock phrase goes, I threw myself on the mercy of the court. What became clear to me, when I later met this image in the Bible, was that throwing myself at the mercy of the court meant throwing myself at the feet of Jesus. The Righteous One stands there in the light of God's favor, in the circle of his approval. He had come at a great price to be with me, to bear the weight of my wrongdoing, so I could share in his justification. He joined me under the judgment of sin, so I could stand with him in the approval of God.

Charles Wesley wonders at this in one of his hymns. He is clearly picturing this great reversal of fortune: in the court of the great King and Judge, he had nothing, until Christ shared with him all the status of God's own vindicated hero. He was condemned, but then suddenly finds himself not merely accepted, but favored. But listen, he says it better:

> No condemnation now I dread; Jesus, and all in him, is mine!
> Alive in him, my living Head, and clothed in righteousness divine,
> Bold I approach the eternal throne, and claim the crown through Christ my own.[2]

THE BEAUTIFUL DEMAND OF TRUST

So how do we accept this provision of righteousness? How do we step into the circle of God's approval? This provision of righteousness is given "to those who believe." So the demanding beauty of this image is that we believe.

Here we need to be careful: By "believe" the Bible never means "understand and agree about the mechanism of justification" or salvation or adoption. It means we *trust* in our Justifier, Savior and Father. Human understanding and mental states are not strong enough to save us—only God is. Trust isn't a mental state; it's a relational state. Trust is a bond between persons. Trusting Jesus means holding on to him and relying on his word that he can see us through on the day of judgment. Our "job" under the new covenant—trust—means we let our voices be still and let his righteousness talk.

That can seem a risky thing to do. There are at least two ways of hanging back from that demanding beauty. One is self-justification, and the other is despair.

FREE FOR GOOD

Angie had built her life in the church very carefully. All children are born with the ability to learn what grownups expect of them, and Angie was not a slow learner. She invested a lot of effort into being a good Christian girl—and she was often proud of how well she did it. But there were times, like at her baptism, that the effort had a frantic edge: How long could she keep this up?

It was a while before she let the mask come off. Finally, during a sermon like many she had heard before, she was ready. She was drawn into the presence of the Judge and found out what she had secretly suspected all along: the mask was worthless. As she dropped her self-justification, the story she told and retold in her own defense, she let herself hear the simple good news: "You don't have to try to be good enough. Jesus already did that for you." Then of course she was free, but not free to run away and be bad. She was free to jump in, free to go and be good.

I saw her later, working hard as a Christian leader. She was doing all the things she had been taught, things that made her folks proud. But she wasn't maintaining a mask; she was laboring in love. She worked hard and laughed often. It's amazing how good you can be when you know you aren't.

YES, YOU

Now back to Tony, sitting at the bar with Jason telling him about God. While Tony felt the distance, the disapproval of God that kept him out, he was not tempted to avoid trust by building a wall of self-defense. He was tempted toward that brand of unbelief called despair: he shied back from trust because he didn't think it would work. He was saying to himself, *That sounds great, but it just won't work for me.* Sure, he looked good to a certain crowd. He was a decent guy, certainly "in" as a varsity athlete. But he knew what he had done to maintain his freedom, and it was more than just hearts broken. One ex-girlfriend he left pregnant, to face an abortion alone. How is God going to take in someone like him? It wasn't going to happen.

But it did. Somehow God made it seem possible. Maybe it was that diagram Jason drew on the napkin, about how everyone is too bad to be with God, but God bridges the gap anyway. Maybe it was Jason's own trust that God could do it, that he could bring Tony in, even that night. Somehow Tony was able to step out of that settled self-judgment of despair and to accept God's judgment in Christ. And he was in.

Now Tony will tell anyone that God can clear their record, that he'll take them in. And he'll show you how, on the back of any napkin you care to give him.

The simple demand of this image is to trust that the goodness Jesus offered for us is enough. Leaning on him, we don't have to worry about where we stand with God—ever.

AS IF, SO THAT

But doubt did creep in on me. After my acquittal in God's court, I was full of joy and I made big changes in my life. But it soon became very clear that I was not perfect yet. In fact, I could still be quite bad.

I was told that being justified meant that God saw me "just-as-if-I'd" been as good as Jesus. But I wasn't really, and I knew it. Maybe I never would be that good. How would he deal with me then?

Sometimes, trying to preserve the fact that we are undeserving of such a gift, Christians preach justification in a way that says "as if, but not really." We emphasize how undeserving we are to be God's people, which is true. But we neglect to say much about how the cross guarantees that we will become fit to be his people. The deepest truth is not that God treats us like the people we are not, but that he treats us as if we are the people that we *soon will be.*

Once I was facing a daughter who was having a meltdown. This happens to all of us at some time, and this was her time. As we spiraled down into a fierce argument that was going nowhere, I could see in her eyes that she wanted out. She was going to be embarrassed about losing her grip, but she could not pull out. She needed help from me. So I just stopped with the judgment and criticism, talked quietly and let her retreat and compose herself. She didn't win the argument. She didn't even apologize. I forget what it was all about, though I'm sure I was in the right. (Aren't we all?) But I had to treat her *as if* she were okay, *so that* she could become okay. And I knew it would work. I was dealing with the girl I knew I would see in an hour, the girl in her right mind. I was treating her as if she were as good as she soon would be.

That's how God was treating me, how he treats everyone he justifies. God has a plan so that these newly justified children of his can grow up to be truly pleasing to him. Paul says, "He condemned sin in human flesh, in order that the righteous requirement of the law might be fully met in us, who do not live according to the sinful nature but according to the Spirit" (Romans 8:3-4 TNIV). I was afraid that he had merely made a change in my heavenly paperwork but I was going to still be as bad as I was. I was afraid the story was forever going to be, "I'll treat you *as if* you are one of my good people, but you aren't really." But the real story was "as if . . . so that." He treated me *as if* I was one of his—he put his Spirit in me—*so that* the Spirit could actually make me righteous.

I can now admit that I have sin in myself, but I can also know it is condemned. The law was right about how I should live, and I will eventually get there. The Spirit of God will bring me.

THERE IS NO DIFFERENCE

The Spirit will bring all of God's people there together. But what happens when you come to the place of acceptance and find some people more accepted than others? What if you came to God's people and found that trusting Jesus wasn't quite enough, that there are more requirements for full membership?

"When I first came here four years ago," Rosa said, "I learned that it wasn't enough for me to love Jesus. I had to check a part of myself at the door to be here. I had to have Jesus *and* to look and talk like you. I did it for a while, but I can't anymore. I am tired, and I have to go."

Rosa had walked into a Christian community on her college campus and found that the circle of God's people was drawn differently than she'd expected. She thought it was about trust in Jesus, but a tighter circle had been drawn. And in that circle, her Latino identity was not welcome.

New Testament scholar N. T. Wright says, "Justification declares that all who belong to Jesus Christ belong at the same table, no matter what their cultural or racial differences."[3] That is no minor corollary of this image; in Paul's hands, this is its major thrust. If you'll count up the instances of justification language in the New Testament, you'll find the majority of them in Romans and Galatians. In those letters Paul is taking careful aim at an issue at the core of the gospel: are Gentile Christians as much God's people as Jewish Christians? And the answer is clear: no other circle may be drawn other than that which God has drawn—trust in Jesus is the only requirement. And, Paul is saying, all of you had better work at sharing that one table.

One Lord, one faith and one new people, for "there is no difference, for all have sinned and fall short of the glory of God, and are justified freely by his grace through the redemption that came by Christ Jesus" (Romans 3:22-23). Do we welcome all who come to us in the name of Jesus? Or are there invisible barriers to those not like us (barriers invisible to us but painfully obvious to those we leave outside)? The Spirit will be at work pulling those down and leading God's people to reach out and embrace those who are different from themselves. If we step into this good news we will know—and be a living display of—the gospel's power.

Where once there was "no one righteous, not even one," now there is a crowd, from every people on earth, gathered around Jesus. Fully secure and approved, confident in the righteousness of Jesus, they welcome in new people every day. God has begun to build his people through faith in Jesus, and he will bring it to its beautiful conclusion. The world needs news as good as this. Let's see they get it.

FORGIVENESS

Picking Up the Bill

The plate smashed on the floor, and my seven-year-old daughter and I both stared at the shattered pieces. I must have looked grumpy as I went for the broom, because she demanded, "Why are you mad? It's not like it's my fault!"

I shot back, in true parental style, "Well, you should have been more careful."

Defying me, she declared, "It doesn't even matter . . . and I'm not sorry!"

My anger flared. "You can just go ahead and pay for it then!"

She broke down. Her face fell and she wailed, "But I can't! That would take all my money! I don't have enough!"

And I melted with her. I held her close and said, "That's all right, hon'. I'll take care of it." Then I got the broom and took care of it.

WHEN BEING SORRY ISN'T ENOUGH

What do you do when you are standing before God, looking at the damage you have caused and knowing that you cannot repair it or repay it? You can feel sad, but the damage has been done. Feeling bad does not change what has happened. And it is not just dinner dishes that are lost; there is real damage all around us:

> The teenage boy finally realizes that God is real and watches over his life. But his life includes episodes where he sexually abused his younger sister. Can he just ride off into the sunset with God, be re-

ligious and forget the past? The reality of what he has done haunts him every time he looks in his sister's eyes.

A father disowns his daughter, refusing to see or speak to her again, and leaves a wound in her soul that bleeds every day. Another father stays with his family, but comes home so drunk on many nights that he staggers in not knowing where he is, sometimes relieving himself on the furniture. How can these men feel better about themselves while they know the damage they have caused in the lives around them?

A young girl tells her brother, "I wish you had never been born," and wrestles for the next twenty years with the anguish of having stabbed so brutally at another heart.

A young man sits alone in a dark apartment, wrestling with his guilt. He told his girlfriend that he loved her, and they declared themselves married and made love that night. But now she is far away and he told her he does not think he can go through with it. He has broken her heart. He couldn't go through with it, but he can't just walk away from it now, either. The damage is much too real and too much his.

We sometimes talk about being "held responsible" for what we have done. We *are* held, connected to our actions and their consequences. What we have done has our name on it, and we must give an account. When the Bible uses the language of forgiveness for what God does, it brings us the idea of accounting and payment. We ask God to "forgive us our debts" because we have many. Our actions have incurred debt with God, far beyond our ability to repay.

SETTLING ACCOUNTS
A debt to God? If I do some wrong to my neighbor or my friend, why does *God* need to forgive me? Isn't it just between us? Why does he need to get involved?

God is very involved. He is connected to his world; he manages and cares for it. When it is wounded, he feels pain; when it is defaced, he is offended; when it is ruined, he rebuilds it. Every life or heart that is shattered by carelessness or greed must be taken care of, and he is the one who does it. The one who cares for the whole world and all the people in it watches over all of the "accounts." All the damage we do, all the cost of our sin, is carried by him—and the charges to our account mount day by day.

Jesus tells us a story about forgiveness in which the one owed is a king. Something like God, any king watches over his whole kingdom. His responsibility covers all the people and their doings. This king decides the time has come for accounts to be settled. All payments due must be made; all debts are called in:

> Therefore, the kingdom of heaven is like a king who wanted to settle accounts with his servants. As he began the settlement, a man who owed him ten thousand talents was brought to him. Since he was not able to pay, the master ordered that he and his wife and his children and all that he had be sold to repay the debt.
>
> The servant fell on his knees before him. "Be patient with me," he begged, "and I will pay back everything." The servant's master took pity on him, canceled the debt and let him go. (Matthew 18:23-27)

Here we see a working man who has accrued millions of dollars in debt. Only gross mismanagement could have resulted in such a huge loss. Millions of dollars that should have been in the king's coffers are missing. He has weakened his king's position, and so the whole kingdom's. But the king has mercy on this servant. Just as I reached out to my daughter, counting her life and happiness as worth far more than a plate, so this king counted this unworthy servant's life as worth more than *ten thousand talents of gold*. That is mercy and grace. That is kindness that brings freedom and a second chance at life. That God should so cover over our mismanagement of our lives is amazing. This is powerful language for the good news.

The parable is not over yet. Jesus is going to be making a point about what forgiveness looks like in our lives. But stopping here for a moment will help us understand forgiveness more clearly and how it tells the gospel story for us.

THE COST OF FORGIVENESS

I've told people the gospel story and then often been asked, If God wanted to forgive us, why didn't he just do it? Why not just drop the issue and let us go on our way? And why this whole business of Jesus dying on the cross? Why does God have to do *that* in order to forgive us? If God is holding a grudge against us, he should just get over it. Let the past be the past.

But understanding the language of forgiveness helps us see that it is not a simple matter of God "getting over" some feelings inside himself. Let's take a look at it: Say a friend owes you a hundred dollars. What does it take you to forgive that friend? You have to make an internal mental decision, yes. Warm feelings help too. But you also have to cover the hundred dollars. That is the cost to you of forgiveness. Like the king who has to absorb millions of dollars of loss as he lets his servant walk away free, you yourself need to make good what is lacking.

Or let's say a college student fools around in school and sends a whole academic year down the tubes. His family can forgive him, but it will cost. Someone will have to pay for another year of college, and the ones who forgive are the ones who will pay.

Let's get more personal. Suppose a friend has insulted you or betrayed your trust. You can forgive her. But it will cost you. You must give up any attempt at getting a payback. You cannot extract special favors out of her through guilt. You cannot humiliate her in turn. And you must put out the effort to continue to treat her as if that event had not happened. Covering over such an offense is costly.

Now suppose that we crush someone with cruelty ("I wish you'd never been born"), break their heart ("I just can't go through with it"), or year by year chip away at their sense of worth ("Oh, you again"). Who can pay the price to restore a heart, a soul, a life? Jesus. He bleeds so that all the people we damage can be whole again. He covers the damage that we couldn't—at the expense of his own life.

And suppose we, as servants of a great king, were given the untold wealth of a whole planet to take care of in his name. What if, through gross mismanagement, we lose ten thousand species, millions of acres, uncounted wonders and opportunities? How could we ever repay such a debt? Somehow Jesus can cover over and make good on what we have lost and wasted. He can restore his whole kingdom, even after our mismanagement. But it will take more than money from his royal treasury. "This is my blood of the covenant, which is poured out for many for the forgiveness of sins" (Matthew 26:28). The king himself must throw his own life into his kingdom so that he might reverse the tide of death and bring creation back to wholeness. He gives his life to sweep up our mess.

The language of forgiveness reminds us that real damage has been done in our sin, and it must be dealt with. It is not only that God's dignity is offended or that some technical regulation has been transgressed. God's dignity is connected to the good of a very real universe. The laws transgressed define what is good and right for very real people and creatures. When those laws are broken, the damage done is real. Someone must pay the price to restore what was ruined. At the cross we see Jesus holding himself responsible for his world and filling in for all that we had broken in it.

So this is the good news, that God has covered over our great debt; he himself has absorbed the cost. In Christ "we have redemption through his blood, the forgiveness of sins, in accordance with the riches of God's grace that he lavished on us with all wisdom and understanding" (Ephesians 1:7-8). The riches of his own life cover over the poverty of ours.

HELD RESPONSIBLE

Ryan was the young man who had promised to be the husband of that young woman—and then left. I sat with him as he clutched his heavy burden in that dark basement apartment. He could feel only the weight and could not see how he could move forward. He had heard that God could forgive, but could he forgive something this real?

Because of the gospel as forgiveness, I could affirm to him that the damage he had caused was real. He felt bad, and I didn't need to explain it away. And we both knew better than to try to believe that God could make it like it had never happened. But I could tell him, "God can lift this burden from you, and he can give you a life-giving way to walk forward." God was not going to undo Ryan's past. He was offering to pour himself into the wounded place so that a new kind of life could grow. And Ryan could walk freely in the kingdom of the forgiven and go about the king's business because the king picked up the burden. But he had to let himself believe that Jesus could actually foot the bill, before he could let himself walk out into the light.

Do you want to know how this story ends? So do I. I carried the proclamation of forgiveness that day, and later our paths diverged. I pray for him, but there was business with God that only he could do.

FACING THE BILL

Strangely, accepting this wonderful offer can be very hard. Every gospel image shows us something like this, a picture of God offering salvation to the world. It also shows how each individual is to accept this word, how he or she is to respond. So how does the image of forgiveness speak "repent and believe"? How does it show how we can enter what God has done for us?

In the parable, the transaction seems fairly straightforward: a request is made and mercy is given. There seems to be no trick to it. However, there is an acknowledgement both parties made before we even hear this conversation. There was an agreement about the situation: The servant had accrued the debt. It was large, and it was his responsibility. There is no debate about the facts, only about what is to be done.

At the end of the age the King will call a general settlement. All the servants will be called in, ready or not, to give account. But now the

King is calling—not compelling—his people to come to settlement. To heed the call and walk into that conversation with the King, we the servants have to acknowledge what is plain on the ledger: we are in deep.

"I'm sorry." "I really did you wrong." "It's my fault." Such simple words that we find so hard to say. As long as we don't say them, though, we are stuck with our responsibility; we are left holding onto a debt load that our souls can't carry.

> If we claim to be without sin, we deceive ourselves and the truth is not in us. If we confess our sins, he is faithful and just and will forgive us our sins and purify us from all unrighteousness. If we claim we have not sinned, we make him out to be a liar and his word has no place in our lives. (1 John 1:8-10)

All we have to do is acknowledge our sins, and we find them forgiven. All the cost of them is gone from us. Why then do we deceive ourselves? Well, why did my daughter refuse any responsibility for the smashed plate? Simple self-defense. Why does "It's not my fault!" spring to our lips so quickly? Because we can't bear the thought that it might be our fault. If the responsibility for *this* lands at my feet, I'm stuck. I'll have to pay big.

I have seen many precious things broken and heard these denials over and over again. I have sat with a group of Christian leaders, the unity of their fellowship shattered by grudges, misunderstanding and distrust. Set faces and smoldering looks were all around—a whole roomful of people who sing about the gospel every week, and no one would own the damage we all could see. All I could hear was people tallying up the charges that others had incurred.

Another room, another time, and I was facing a married couple. He sat at one end of the table, she at the other, and they seldom looked at each other as they spoke. I have talked with too many couples in strained and broken marriages and, while the wreckage is strewn all over the house, seldom does anyone claim it. It's simply too dangerous. If you admit your responsibility, you pay. In money or effort or shame, you pay.

That's the law we live under in this world. And we often project onto God that unwillingness to forgive.

Often we can only imagine him dealing with us only the way people do—using our indebtedness against us. Sure, he'll "forgive" us, but it will be clear that we owe him. We'll have to reform and repay. We'll have to be good to make up for being bad. We and all we have will be sold (probably to the church) to pay our debt. God will have the upper hand and will dictate our lives to us. He will not really release us; we will be in debt forever.

If this is how we see the deal, if this is the picture lurking in the back of our minds, no wonder many of us shy away. We don't see freedom from that settlement, just shame and bondage. We don't really think we'll be released, so we won't come and admit our debt. In other words, we don't repent because we don't believe.

PREEMPTIVE FORGIVENESS

But the beautiful thing about God's forgiveness is that it is given even before we ask. The outcome of the settlement is sure before we even walk in the door. If fact, we are called in expressly to be freed. This goes against what we might expect from life or even from this particular parable. (If any one image of the gospel can have flat sides and mislead if we are not careful, then one telling of one image must be even more limited.)

From this parable we might think that the servant's asking prompted the king's forgiveness. This would be a story we are used to: the well-crafted apology wins over the reluctant forgiveness. I have crafted some very careful apologies in my day and done some very good pleading. And it sometimes "works." So it is tempting for me to read this pattern into God's forgiveness. We servants might do such a great job of begging and looking pitiful that it melts the king's heart. But it is not so in the gospel. It is the *King's* action that melts *our* hearts. It's "God's kindness [that] leads you toward repentance" (Romans 2:4).

The action he takes is forgiveness, and our response is to believe and receive. John Calvin is thought of as preaching a stern version of Christianity, but he saw that God leads us with kindness. He spoke clearly of how God does not wait for us to repent before he forgives: "Repentance is not made a condition in such a sense as to be a foundation for meriting pardon," but instead God "resolved to take pity on men for the express purpose of leading them to repent."[1] We have to turn from our sins in order to please him, but he makes it possible by first showing us his gracious forgiveness. This healthy repentance "we see in all those who, first stung with a sense of sin, but afterwards raised and revived by confidence in the divine mercy, turned to the Lord."[2] He first turns to us with forgiveness in hand, then we turn to him in response.

So forgiveness is proclaimed, and we are invited in; "through Jesus the forgiveness of sins is proclaimed to you" (Acts 13:38). This good news comes to us while we are still in our defensiveness and our denial. It tells us the sure outcome if we step into that settlement. Forgiveness already granted gives us the freedom to ask. This image demands that we admit our great debt, but his prepayment on the cross makes it safe for us to admit what we owe.

Preaching His Kindness

When Christians give the gospel word, we can be afraid to be as generous as God. We are afraid, perhaps like parents, to let people off too lightly. "Well, you should have been more careful" feels better. Perhaps we are afraid that if we say, "Don't worry, he'll take care of it," people won't really admit their sin and be forgiven. So we press for the admission, for people to feel the extent of their debt.

But once that plate had smashed on the floor, if I had started off with "It's okay, I'll take care of it," I think I would've been more likely—not less—to hear "I'm sorry." And I might even have gotten some help in cleaning up.

So we proclaim forgiveness as a done deal and call people to believe and step into it. We command them to come to settlement, ordering them with royal authority to ask for the release that has already been granted.

THE CONDITION OF FORGIVENESS

All this freedom—is there a catch? Well, yes, there seems to be. When Jesus teaches his disciples to pray, one of the few elements included is forgiveness, and its condition: "Forgive us our sins, for we ourselves forgive everyone indebted to us" (Luke 11:4 NRSV; see also Matthew 6:12). The Lord is insistent on this point: "When you stand praying, if you hold anything against anyone, forgive him, so that your Father in heaven may forgive you your sins" (Mark 11:25).

This is a hard condition. If admitting that we are debtors is hard enough, this is worse. What is harder than forgiving someone who has done us wrong? I am not talking about excusing things that weren't their fault; I am talking about forgiveness. What they did to us was wrong, and they knew it. Yet still we must forgive, or we will receive no forgiveness.

How is this a gospel of grace? Must sinners first do that hardest of all acts of love, forgiving those who hurt us, before we can enter into God's good graces? It doesn't seem possible, so it's good that this is not what is being asked of us. Forgiving others isn't what we do to become worthy of forgiveness. It is the mark that we are willing to accept forgiveness.

We can see this as we let the Lord's parable of the unmerciful servant unfold. That first forgiveness of the king was just the beginning. That great mercy seems to be merely the backdrop, or the foundation, of the rest. The heart of the story is still to come. What happens, or should have happened, as a result of the king's mercy seems to be all the point.

But when that servant went out, he found one of his fellow servants who owed him a hundred denarii. He grabbed him and began to choke him. "Pay back what you owe me!" he demanded.

His fellow servant fell to his knees and begged him, "Be patient with me, and I will pay you back."

But he refused. Instead, he went off and had the man thrown into prison until he could pay the debt. When the other servants saw what had happened, they were greatly distressed and went and told their master everything that had happened.

Then the master called the servant in. "You wicked servant,' he said, 'I canceled all that debt of yours because you begged me to. Shouldn't you have had mercy on your fellow servant just as I had on you?" In anger his master turned him over to the jailers to be tortured, until he should pay back all he owed.

This is how my heavenly Father will treat each of you unless you forgive your brother from your heart. (Matthew 18:28-35)

This man who has been welcomed into forgiveness does not have forgiveness in himself. He will not offer it. This endangers his fellow servant. It "greatly distresses" those around him. And it provokes the king who had forgiven him. There is a sense of outrage here, of offense. There has been a breach of trust, a betrayal. The king had brought this man in, he had covered over his debts, he had poured out his own resources to lift this man up and enable him to remain a part of the kingdom. But the servant offends against forgiveness. He abuses and even defies the way of the king. He walks around bringing ruin on his fellow servants and dishonor to the king who forgave him.

So the king hands the servant over to his own rejection of forgiveness. He is thrown back into the realm were he is held responsible for his own actions. Reject the way of forgiveness and there is nothing left to do— but pay.

This story shows forgiveness to be more than a one-time transaction. Jesus begins this parable by saying, "The kingdom of heaven is like . . ." It seems we are not offered a one-time covering over of debts, but rather an entrance into the kingdom where forgiveness reigns.

FORGIVENESS ON US ALL

Let's go back to the woman disowned by her father. At twenty, Flora had begun to take stock of her life and realized that her father had been abusive toward her. (When we are damaged as children, it often takes years to figure out that the pain we grew up with is not normal.) While she was taking stock of the wreckage, she had an argument with him, and she laid the charge of the damage at his feet. He not only refused any responsibility, he cut off relationship on the spot—and hasn't spoken to her since.

He refused to take any responsibility for his debt, but the Lord took care of things anyway. I have watched the King of forgiveness pour his own life into hers so that the brokenness could be healed and turned into new strength. The past is still there; it is often only through tears that I have heard her say, "Jesus is being so good to me." But God is making good on the debt, as he always does.

My friend has received forgiveness of her own sins from Jesus, and that of course is another story. But she knows she lives in the kingdom where forgiveness reigns, and she accepts the law of forgiveness. So she has held out her hands to her father and offered forgiveness to him. Though Jesus has covered over the debt he incurred, he still remains aloof. But Flora continues to stand with God, agreeing with him about her father's forgiveness. She is living in the good news and hoping he will join her soon.

A KINGDOM OF RELEASE

We are called into a kingdom where the rule is forgiveness. This helps make sense of what we heard John say earlier: "If we confess our sins, he is faithful and just and will forgive us our sins and purify us from all unrighteousness." It seemed simple at first, but read it again, and wonder why is he "faithful and just" to forgive our sins.

I would have said, "He is good and kind and will forgive our sins" or maybe "He is merciful and gracious and will forgive." But faithful and just? What do these have to do with forgiveness? Then I remembered that the writer, though he writes in simple Greek, is a Jew. He knows the King of Israel, the God of covenant faithfulness. Faithfulness and justice are covenant terms. John is thinking of that King upholding his covenant duty to his people: they come to him in need, and he cares for them. He is faithful and just—that is, he upholds his part in his relationship with his people. His part as the good King is to use his resources to cover the need of his people.

In entering his court, we are entering a place of forgiveness. His kingdom is a place where all debts are released. If we come there, then, we have to agree with the Lord's decision, his way of running his kingdom. And release from debts is the law. Accepting your own forgiveness means accepting everyone's. When a believer stands and prays, "Forgive us our debts as we forgive our debtors," she is saying. "Here I am, still accepting that you forgive us all. Keep forgiving me too."

Deny your neighbor's forgiveness and you have stepped outside the covenant; you have rejected the King's decision; you have left the place of forgiveness. Accept your neighbor's forgiveness and enter a place of complete freedom. That freedom looks like good news that we have needed for a long time.

AS WE FORGIVE THOSE

Do you recall the brother and sister, the abuser and the abused? I saw them stand together and testify to the forgiveness of God. The brother stood before a group of people and told of the hideous thing he had done. The crowd was absolutely still as he began to unfold the story. (How could he have done that? How could he be facing us and admitting it?) But he forged on with his story: "And I had to face God . . . and he told me he could even handle what I had done. And he had me." The tension drained away; grace could cover over even this.

Then the sister, now a grown woman, came up to testify. And I was afraid. Was I going to hear a shallow "everything's alright now" from a woman who was told she had to forgive because it was the Christian thing to do? Was I going to see a sweet smile from a woman abused by her religion now, instead of just her brother? I watched closely as she spoke and began to be amazed. I saw nothing forced—her face was beautiful to look at. She was not burdened in any way. She wasn't making herself be a good girl—she was just . . . free.

And I realized I hadn't believed in God's forgiveness, at least not enough. I had believed he could forgive a lot of sins but not *this*. The reality of forgiveness was too big even for me, a sometime preacher of the gospel. The beauty of that kingdom is dazzling, the grace of the King limitless. And for those two, standing there and holding hands, it meant much more than any record of past evil and brokenness. The King had put his own life in to cover theirs, and it had turned out to be far more than enough.

Through the lens of forgiveness, we see a gospel that deals squarely with the reality of evil and the damage it causes. Wrong isn't ignored; nothing is swept under the rug. The full price is always paid, full restoration is always made, everything is made right—by him. And we walk free, forgiving as we are forgiven, nothing keeping us from life in his new kingdom. There is nothing this good news can't handle.

ATONEMENT

Taking Away Our Shame

The man and the woman covered themselves and hid. Their beautiful life had suddenly gone very horribly wrong, and they knew they themselves were the problem.

This is the old story of our first parents in the Garden and the eating of the forbidden fruit. Look at that story and notice: when they had gone against God's command and eaten that fruit, there is no talk about them hiding the evidence of the deed. There is no attempt to bury the apple core. What they hid was themselves. They couldn't bear to be naked in front of each other anymore, and they hid away when God came.

And so our race learned about shame. We know there is something about us that we need to hide. We are somehow defective, gross, unseemly. We hang our heads, knowing we are less than we ought to be.

Shame is the flip side of guilt. Our culture is more used to thinking about guilt than shame, though recently both psychologists and theologians have been doing some very helpful work with both. One simple way to understand guilt and shame is this: Guilt looks out at the damage we have done. Shame looks in and says, "Who *are* you, that you could have done such a thing?"[1]

A friend of mine relates a time when he had given in to the pull of pornography on the Internet and had accidentally left it on the screen for his son to come in and see. He did not just feel that he had done a wrong act; he suddenly felt exposed. Something ugly about him had just become as plain as day—to one of the last people he ever wanted to see it.

He felt shame, and he wished the whole house could have fallen on him to cover him up.

SHAME—TRUE AND FALSE

I want to be clear as I start talking about shame. Shame is not just a feeling. In popular use, shame is now the enemy of a healthy self-image. It is something to be eradicated so we might be happier people. Now only old ladies in movies can be heard saying, "Have you no shame?" We are more likely to be heard saying, "Have you no self-respect?" But in an effort to avoid the unhealthy aspects of shame, something useful has been lost.

We can get a clearer idea of shame if we stop and look at how we think about guilt. We often mark the difference between real (or objective) guilt and feelings of guilt. *Guilt* is the fact of our having done this or that wrong, while *guilt feelings* come from our perception of wrongdoing. Let's say I have done wrong. I might feel that I have done wrong, or I might not. Perhaps my wrong was in the past and I have "gotten over it." This does not make me less guilty; I just feel that way. But now let's suppose I have been mistreated and I feel that something was my fault when it wasn't. Then I have guilt feelings, but they are baseless, false. Guilt and guilt feelings can be connected, but they are not the same.

Actual guilt, when we recognize it, should produce feelings in us that move us to action. False guilt, untrue accusations living in our hearts, can also stir up feelings in us. The charges of false guilt must be disproved and the feelings denied. The charges of real guilt must be faced and the feelings listened to, so that we might deal with the problem.

So, too, with shame. Shame deals not with what we have done but with what we are. There are realities about our selves as well as feelings about ourselves. My friend whose porn use was exposed felt ashamed. He had shame feelings, and those feelings were a proper response to the reality of a shameful truth about his soul. Of course, he is not alone; there are real things wrong with all of us.

Yes, there are also many false things we are told about ourselves. Voices from the media, our peers, even our families can give us untrue messages. These can provoke in us very harmful thoughts, false feelings of shame that must be dealt with. But what of the real ugliness in our souls? What of the real pettiness out of which flow all our individual petty acts. What about the lust, jealousy and greed we can usually hide, but which we know is ours night and day? If we call all our feelings about those things unreal and try to conjure them away with misguided therapy, we will not be better people. Either the attempt will fail and we will be tempted to despair, or it will succeed and we will become shameless, which is not a good thing at all. We must trace down feelings of shame to their root and see ourselves for who we truly are.

SHAME SPEAKS

Shame signals there is something wrong in our souls, our communities, even our bodies. Like pain, these feelings tell us something is terribly wrong. The burden felt by our first parents is still with us. We feel it on every level of our lives.

When I was thirteen, going to the pool was both a treat and a torture. Overweight, with my back covered with acne, I could hardly bear to be seen. But I also couldn't bear to be left out. So I went but covered up my gross self as much as possible. On the physical level, in our bodies, we feel that we are not right. We are slack-bodied and feel that it shows our laziness. Some of us have been marred by disease, some shortchanged by genetics. We often feel—not evil—but awkward, unlovely. We are an embarrassment to be seen, and to see. Even if we could erase all the unreal standards of beauty thrown at us by the media, we would still feel it—something is not right with us. If nothing else, old age takes away our beauty, our strength and even our minds. Something is wrong in the world and it has touched even my body, and I want to cover up.

Then there is shame that goes deeper. Cindy hung around our Christian fellowship, often at the fringes of any event. I can see her now, tentatively looking around to make sure it was okay for her to be there, half of the time hiding behind her hair. I don't know where she felt her lack or what messages had come to her. Whatever it was, it was deep; she didn't feel she could really come out into the open with people or with God. "I mean, you're good people; I can tell. I just don't think I can be like you. . . . It would be nice though." She longed to come out and walk with God, but didn't see a way.

Not only in our own souls, but also in the souls of our families and communities we feel the gap. Mom or Dad is an alcoholic—and the children feel shame. No, it's not the kids' fault, but there is a real sickness that they are truly connected to. It affects them and they feel that unwholesome connection. So they hide, saying, "I just don't invite people over." But what they're really saying is "Don't look. We're ugly if you look too close."

Even at a national level we feel the difference between our best self— the identity we hope for—and the one that too often gets exposed. The scandals come and the anthems sound that much more hollow. We see ourselves from a new perspective, and it doesn't look pretty.

I was relaxing once with some colleagues, chatting casually about the upcoming holidays. We were asking each other playfully what was on our Christmas wish lists. One couple was silent. We asked if they were okay. "We just got back from Nicaragua. . . . We're not ready to talk about Christmas yet, all right?" and they looked down. After seeing the need of the world, our nation's materialistic glory seemed shameful to them. Our hearts echo Isaiah's words: "Woe to me! . . . For I am a man of unclean lips, and I live among a people of unclean lips, and my eyes have seen the King, LORD Almighty" (Isaiah 6:5). We the people become exposed and don't feel pride.

At every level we feel the ruin of ourselves. We are unpresentable, and we know it.

RECOVERING THE IMAGE

But there is good news for those of us who have a sense that we are less than we should be, for those of us who feel shame, who know there is something about us that can't bear to be brought out in the open. The gospel image of atonement is one that helps us very clearly here.

I have to stop again to make sure we are clear about terms. Popular use in church circles has *atonement* standing for what God did in paying for our sins. I suppose we have to use some word. I myself will often use *salvation* in this book to stand for all of what God has done for us in Jesus. I do this knowing that *salvation* is also a very sharp and concrete term for a rescue; left to its original meaning it can speak to me a clear word, a unique contribution to my overall vision of what God has done. So, too, with *atonement*. The New Testament writers don't use it as their overall word for what happened at the cross; it comes up in a few places, always associated with a reference to the temple sacrifices. I want to get back to this use of the word. I want to allow atonement language to paint its own distinctive image of what God has done for us.

And it is quite a unique picture: atonement brings us to the realm of the temple and of ritual sacrifices. This is not a daily reality for us, like debt or a law court might be. It feels more like a great scene from a movie, with costumes and altars, smoke and chanting. But this can still serve us well; the feeling of high drama is appropriate. The sacrifices in the temple were a great drama also for the people of Israel. It wasn't daily life for them either. It was a passion play enacted in their culture before they knew whose passion was being spoken of. To understand all this rightly, though, we have to go back to before religion was even invented.

OFFERING OUR SELVES

We need to go back to the Garden, where it was simply God and his people. There was no religion there, just life. God came to his people, and they came to him, and they walked together "in the cool of the day" (Genesis 3:8). God came and offered his children his own presence, and they came to him with their offering: simply themselves. Before God and each other they were naked and unashamed. And it was good.

When the man and the woman rebelled, however, all this was broken. They not only realized they were naked, they also knew they didn't want to be. And so they covered up. Their good and proper offering to God had been their own selves, but now those selves weren't fit to be seen.

Even then, God helped cover over these lives that were no longer fit to be offered to him. After he had told them the results of their disobedience, he provided the skins of animals for them to cover themselves. Already another living thing was paying for us; another was paying the price to cover over what we could not bear to have exposed.

OFFERING A LIFE

While the man and the woman and their descendants labored in the world, making their way along and carrying the burden of their shame, God readied the cure. His work with Israel was a part of his plan. When he brought the people of Israel up out of Egypt, he told them how to live with him as his people. He gave them the moral law, which taught them how to be good. They were to do business fairly, be good to foreigners, take care of widows and never lie or steal or murder. Act like this, and they would have nothing to hide. But it was a given: they would break that law. So he also gave them the temple system to deal with the fact of their sin. This system of law and sacrifice was a gift to the people. It taught them what good life was, how they fell short of it and how God would take care of them when they did fall short.

PICTURING WHAT'S WRONG

And the picture is clear. How far they have come from the Garden! No longer are they living in Eden, walking with God in the cool of the day. Now they are huddled in the midst of the wilderness, their camp encircling the Tent of Meeting, the place of God's presence. But as the camp crowds around their Maker and Savior, they are also cut off from him. Great curtains separate them from his presence. And even the high priest dare not go into the Most Holy Place but once a year, and then only with blood. "The LORD said to Moses: 'Tell your brother Aaron not to come whenever he chooses into the Most Holy Place behind the curtain in front of the atonement cover on the ark, or else he will die, because I appear in the cloud over the atonement cover'" (Leviticus 16:2). This people is gathered around their God and Savior, but can't come too close—

not because they are humans and he is God, but because something is wrong with them.

The problem is moral guilt, and more. Sacrifices were necessary to atone for what we would call sins and crimes, but also for other kinds of "uncleanness." Houses that had mildew, people who had skin diseases, and even women who had their normal periods—all were unclean. All these had to be "atoned for" with sacrifice and blood. What's more, the proper offerings for the woman after her period and the person after the skin disease were called "sin" and "guilt" offerings (for examples of these, see Leviticus 13:7; 14:19, 53; 15:15; 16:30). Clearly the people are being given a picture of sin that was deeper than accountability for specific breaches of the law. They are being reminded of a deep reality: among them was a pervasive problem that affected all they did and touched.

The most poignant image of this uncleanness was the leper. We read in the Law, "The person with such an infectious disease must wear torn clothes, let his hair be unkempt, cover the lower part of his face and cry out, 'Unclean! Unclean!' As long as he has the infection he remains unclean. He must live alone; he must live outside the camp" (Leviticus 13:45-46). Outside the camp, away from God and his people, he is ordered to be ugly and cry out, "There is something wrong with me!" This is what it means to be unclean.

THERE IS SOMETHING WRONG WITH ME

Alan had the look of shame: he kept looking down at the table instead of at me. Physically he was there with God's people, but in his heart he was outside the camp, and a voice in his mind was crying out, "Unclean! Unclean!" He couldn't shake the feeling that he shouldn't be welcomed by God or his people. "I hear that God loves me, but I just can't take it in. I can't." Somewhere in his past he had been told that he was a mess, a disappointment, that there was something wrong with him.

My friend Stan, who had left that porn on his computer screen, didn't have vague notions that he was unworthy. He knew he had something gross about him, something he didn't want brought into the light. He could say very clearly, "There is something wrong with me!"

Whether it is a vague sense of unworthiness, a label put on us by others or a real knowledge of our flaws, we have to deal with the sense there is something wrong with us. And God has given us an image of how he deals with it.

POINTING TOWARD HOPE

Suppose these two men I know lived in ancient Israel. How would they see God deal with their sin and shame? They would bring an animal as an offering to "make atonement." They would know this sacrifice would do two things for them as worshipers: it would offer life to God, and it would bear away sin.

Sometimes we talk as if the death of the sacrifice were a punishment for the crime of sin. But the language of punishment is absent here. We must let this image speak its own message clearly. The life is not taken by God at the altar—in vengeance or punishment—*it is offered by the people*. In his overview of classic Christianity, Thomas Oden sums it up this way: "Essentially the sacrifice was a human gift to God, presented by those aware of their sins and hoping that the severity of divine holiness might be turned to clemency."[2]

Now, back to our two burdened worshipers in ancient Israel. They are aware of their sins and are going to make an offering to God. What would the offering teach them even as they did it? The key is God's requirement that the animal they present be perfect, free from any blemish. They would have to get the best they had and inspect it carefully. But this was not because God was simply picky. The spotless animal reminds them what God had intended for their lives. Their duty and joy was to come and offer back to him the beautiful, clean lives they had been given. The Law had described how he wanted their lives to look. It was reminding them of who he created them to be back in the Garden: the people who could offer themselves to him in good conscience. They were to "be holy, because I am holy" (Leviticus 11:44-45; see also 19:2; 20:7).

But they had sinned, and so the offering of their blemished lives was displeasing to God. It provoked anger, not pleasure, in him. They owed him a clean life but had none to give. So that's why they were told to bring this perfect animal as an offering instead, in place of their own. As they lead in this prize animal, it reminds them that only a perfect life, wholly and completely given, would be pleasing to God. The death itself was not what is pleasing to him; it was merely the way to give God the whole life of the animal, "for the life of a creature is in the blood, and I have given it to you to make atonement for yourselves on the altar; it is the blood that makes atonement for one's life" (Leviticus 17:11). And the good life of the sacrifice would take the place of their flawed life.

As these burdened people watch the priests take the life of this animal, they know that God's anger has turned away from them. He was angry at the offering of an imperfect life, but now he has been offered a good and pleasing life; his demand has been satisfied and he is well pleased. The offering goes up in smoke as "an aroma pleasing to the LORD" (Leviticus 1:9).

So our two friends would see the pleasing offering made, but they would also know that their sin is taken away: after the blood and the appropriate body parts were offered on the altar, the rest of the carcass was taken and burned outside the camp (see Leviticus 4:11-12, 21). A perfect offering for their lives has pleased God, and their shame has been disposed of. Now our friends can go home in peace.

This was played out again and again for individuals, but the whole nation also saw these two things once a year, on the Day of Atonement. On that one day alone, the priest was to go into the Most Holy Place, and he went there with the blood of an unblemished goat. But the sacrifice that day also had another goat. This goat was to bear away the sins of the people. The leaders laid their hands on the head of the goat and confessed the sins of the people, and then the goat was driven away into the desert, bearing the sins of the people with it. So, in this sacrifice, all the people would see the two solutions of God clearly. He will find a way to give the people a clean offering to make, and he will take away their sins.

THE TRUE OFFERING

All this was ritual done in hope. Animal stand-ins could be no more than placeholders. In all the centuries in which the sacrifice was enacted, no one could manage to bring God more than that symbol of a perfect life—until Jesus. The writer of Hebrews reminds us that the sacrifices of Israel were a symbol of what was to come, but the reality was Jesus: "How much more, then, will the blood of Christ, who through the eternal Spirit offered himself unblemished to God, cleanse our consciences from acts that lead to death, so that we may serve the living God!" (9:14).

Here is an offering that gives real cleansing. (Sanctification, the imagery of cleansing, here fills out the atonement image. It shows us being made clean and holy.) When Jesus gives his life, the cleansing goes deep, and our conscience ends up spotless and free. That voice inside us, crying out in anguish, "Unclean! Unclean!" can be stilled. We can walk away from that offering knowing that we are pleasing in God's sight.

To win this for us Jesus offered "his blood"—his life. Remember, "the life of a creature is in the blood." Jesus prepared a perfect offering for his Father—his own body, his own life. Day by day, through all his years in this fallen world, he crafted a perfect human life, then "he offered himself unblemished to God." The eternal Son of God became the human Son of God, a proper offering from humanity to God. He brought what we could not: a good human life.

And he brought himself. He is pictured both as the acceptable priest, bringing the offering, and as the acceptable offering itself. Here we feel that things have been finally healed and made whole. The real life behind the religious ritual is now coming together again. No longer do we bring an animal's life, using something outside ourselves, as a symbol of our life. Back in the Garden, both the man and the woman were like Jesus; they brought themselves as their offering. Now again, Jesus is both the bringer and the brought. It is good and right and natural—a person coming to God and saying, "Here I am."

And we can come to God in him. This ancient imagery offers real people vital help today. Alan had trouble believing God could accept and love him. But he could see that the perfect offering of Jesus was "a new and living way" to God (Hebrews 10:20). And he took it. But that did not mean that he was through with this image. Shame issues run deep, and Alan will cling to this telling of the gospel for a long time.

Eventually Alan got into counseling. When deep past and family issues are involved, people wise in the ways of the human heart can be a great help. Alan had a lot of lies in his soul, false feelings of shame for things that weren't true or weren't his fault. But the gospel was still medicine he needed for two reasons. First, whether or not the voices in his head were true, he still needed to fight them. Sometimes he had the strength to say, "That's a lie! In Jesus, I am good enough to go to God." But other times he wasn't strong enough or became confused. At those times he clung to "even if that's true, Jesus is truer. He's good and the Father loves him. And me too." This image can help so many break through the wall of shame and "approach the throne of grace with confidence, so that we may receive mercy and find grace to help us in our time of need" (Hebrews 4:16).

Alan also needed this word because, as the lies were being exposed, new ugly truths were found. The lies of false shame often feed off things in us we know are wrong. Sometimes they are even harder to face than the old familiar shame. But Jesus covers over all. He has power not only to dispel lies but also to save us from the real diseases of our souls.

BEARING OUR SHAME

Jesus bears away our real sin and its shame. That's the only reason Stan and I could talk so freely about the porn incident.

Jesus not only made the good offering we couldn't, he also takes our place "outside the camp." He bears away our sin; he is thrown out as unclean. Listen as the author of Hebrews portrays Jesus for us: "The high priest carries the blood of animals into the Most Holy Place as a sin offering, but the bodies are burned outside the camp. And so Jesus also suffered outside the city gate to make the people holy through his own blood" (13:11-12). Jesus bears our disgrace; he is thrown out as unclean even as he makes us clean.

Crucifixion was a shameful, as well as painful, death. And Paul says, "I have been crucified with Christ and I no longer live, but Christ lives in me" (Galatians 2:20).[3] So the Stan that had visited that porn site died on the cross with Jesus. That part of his self is borne away with the death of Jesus. The person who did that was not the real Stan, but the Stan who is passing away. The acceptable-in-Christ Stan is the real Stan. So I talked with a man who was "real" about his sin, but we both knew what was more real was the beautiful life he had in Jesus.

No More Hiding

So this image calls us to come out of hiding, to believe that God will accept us now, to come with confidence into God's presence: "Therefore, brothers, since we have confidence to enter the Most Holy Place by the blood of Jesus, by a new and living way opened for us through the curtain, that is, his body, and since we have a great priest over the house of God, let us draw near to God with a sincere heart in full assurance of faith" (Hebrews 10:19-22).

No shame need hold us back. With Jesus' death, the temple curtain was torn open (see Mark 15:38), so "let us then approach the throne of grace with confidence." We don't need to hide in the bushes, like Adam and Eve, any longer. In Jesus, we are as beautiful to God as his own perfect Son. His goodness is offered for us and brings us in so we can find the mercy and grace we need.

Making It Simple

So we've gone the whole journey of this gospel image, from the Garden through ancient Israel to Jesus. I went the long way around to better give you the full impact of this image. But this gospel truth need not weave its way through the temple every time we tell it. Remember, it is a story of life and how life ought to be; it is a story of our shame and how our shame is taken away.

In the Garden, it was simply life—God offering himself to us and us offering ourselves to God. Jesus comes to restore that openness before God. We don't need to hide; we can come to him. We can come to him and he will be pleased.

Again, let's go back to one of the first pictures we see of Jesus. When John baptized the people in the wilderness, all the people came and confessed their sins. They were being baptized to show that they acknowledged that they needed to be cleansed—because the actions that flowed from their heart showed that they were deeply dirty, shameful. But when Jesus comes and rises up out of the water, God says, "You are my son, whom I love; with you I am well pleased" (Mark 1:11). The offering was good and acceptable. When Jesus finished his life, he told his Father, "Into your hands I commit my spirit" (Luke 23:46), and the Father received the offering of his life. To be "in Jesus" in this image is to be able to stand right beside Jesus, look up to heaven with him, and see God smiling down on the offering of your life and saying, "With you I am well pleased." That is good news.

And Christians have always known it, even when we lose the crystal-clear sharpness of this image. We've always known the gospel went deeper than a mere clearing of the penalty for sins. It goes down to who we really are. How many times have you heard the gospel spoken as this: "It's okay that you are not good enough. God knows that. He sent Jesus to be good enough for you." It's that simple, that deep and that needed by so many of us.

CONFIDENCE TO APPROACH THE THRONE

Remember my friend Cindy, who hung at the edges of our group? Like so many shy people, she wanted to come out and offer herself but just couldn't. Afraid to be noticed, but afraid to be alone—ever since the Garden there is a part of all of us peering out from the undergrowth, both hoping and fearing to be found.

Of course she heard the word of God's acceptance spoken by us, but the biggest thing was that she saw the face of his acceptance. By welcoming her throughout the whole year, we "preached" to her that she was acceptable to us. The beauty of Jesus' life has opened a new and living way to God, and it lived in that fellowship. This rich and complex gospel image, this life-giving word, can come through so simply: We are so glad you're here. You are not just acceptable; you are pleasing, even delightful.

And she was drawn. She let herself get involved in a Bible study of the Gospels and saw this man Jesus, and let herself be brought in by him. "He was—is—just so amazing! It's not my stuff that matters. It's about him!" How wonderful, then, that this thing that is "all about him" helped her brighten up, become free and more herself than ever. When Jesus takes away our shame, he uncovers our real self in him.

CALLED OUT OF HIDING

When I was in second grade, we all had little individual desks with a storage area under the desktop. One day I got a paper with a poor grade on it. I couldn't bear to bring it home, so I jammed it into my desk, all the way to the back.

It must have been a bad year, or maybe hiding once made it easier to do it again, because after a few weeks my desk was full of papers stuffed toward the back. They sat there in the dark, and no one knew. I, myself, wasn't even quite sure what was in there. But the truth comes out—my mom asked the teacher one day why I wasn't bringing any work home.

So the teacher came over to me the next day and asked if she could look into my desk. We unpacked it, one awful paper at a time. I have to say I didn't feel like I was being saved that morning; it felt like public torture. I would have much preferred to stay on the comfortable path to academic oblivion. But the desk got unpacked, and I was straightened out—sweaty and embarrassed but really none the worse for wear.

If we are to let Jesus bear away our shame, we'll have to let him see it and get hold of it. Admitting these things, bringing them into the light and being brave enough to move forward with the cleaning—all this is part of the demanding beauty of this image.

If we claim to be without sin, we deceive ourselves and the truth is not in us. If we confess our sins, he is faithful and just and will forgive us our sins and purify us from all unrighteousness. . . . He is the atoning sacrifice for our sins, and not only for ours but also for the sins of the whole world. (1 John 1:8-9; 2:2)

In Jesus we can live out—and speak out—the truth that there is a new and living way back to the throne of grace. Jesus offering himself covers all of us. Now to God you are as acceptable—no, as beautiful—as Jesus.

That is the good news that the sacrifice of atonement brings us back to. Our shame is taken away. We can come out of hiding. Our Maker will come to us, and we will offer ourselves to him, clean in Jesus. So we will walk together in the cool of the day, and it will be very good.

part 3

IMAGES OF DELIVERANCE

We started by looking at images of life, what God is bringing us into. Then our second set of images began to show us how God clears the way. He deals with the evil inside us, so that he might bring us into his new life. But salvation is played out on a bigger stage than the one that displays our own good and bad decisions. Not all of the obstacles are inside us.

While affluent people and societies can temporarily forget, most of the world knows they are not in control of their destinies. They live much of their lives under the power of others. And those aware of the spiritual side of life know that not all of the powers out there are human; there are spiritual forces against us. Even people who are materially well off can wake up to the fact that they are not in control, that their lives are hemmed in by a bent world, and even that their own wills won't always obey them. We need rescue and, when we look, we find God strong for us.

SALVATION

The Mighty Hand of God

I was a prostitute and a crack addict," she declared. "I was so messed up, the state came and took away my babies. I couldn't be with my own children no more 'cause I couldn't be a good mother." The crowd listened, and gave her words of encouragement to go on. It was testimony time at a downtown African American church service. The woman went on: "And then the church reached out to me. I came in and they loved me, and I found God. And, you know, he delivered me. He saved me out of prostitution and drugs, and he gave me a new life." Clapping and amens started coming, a "glory to God!" came from the back. "Now I'm standing here among you with my *husband*, and last week we heard that the state is going to give me back my babies. They're coming home. Praise God!"

Most of her story wasn't news to her congregation. But they still greeted it with smiles and shouts of praise; they loved hearing and celebrating it again. And the form she told it in was tried and true. It was a distinct genre, a part of their community's liturgy—a testimony to God's power. These people knew how to tell—and to hear—stories of God's saving power. They lived in the care of a God who saves. Even their church's name spoke what the gospel was to them: Dynamic Deliverance.

NEEDING RESCUE

Deliverance, rescue, salvation. The New Testament uses this set of terms more than all the others we have seen so far. So it's no wonder Christians often talk of being "saved"; it's all over the Bible. But "getting saved" now sounds like a quaint, old-time formula or like a synonym for "becoming religious." But that's not what believers through the centuries have meant when they said God is a savior. What they mean is that he is one who comes to help his people, one who hears when they are oppressed or overwhelmed, one who acts on their behalf.

Even in our culture of unprecedented power and affluence, many are calling out in desperation. Carol was a teenage girl who, like many, was haunted by hurts and doubts, and would often withdraw to her room for comfort. She was into lots of hard rock and roll; she idolized the stars and drank in their message, destructive as it often was. Her refuge became a fearful place, though, when she began to feel other presences with her in the dark. When demonic faces began to peer out of the posters on the wall, it was clear she needed help from somewhere, and she began to call on God

Ellen was a young woman studying in Europe who had chosen to let her Christian life fade into the background. Thinking of all that God had "let happen" in her life and not feeling very close to God in the present, she let herself get into an intimate and very unhealthy relationship with a man. One day she took stock of her situation, and what she saw in her own heart scared her. Her bitterness was building a trap for her. "I saw that if I kept going, I could become a witch. Not the magic kind—I mean, I saw myself becoming a hard, mean woman, with hatred deep inside. I saw it; I could go there. I *was* going there. And I didn't know if I could stop. So I called out, 'God! You've got to stop me!'"

Even though he was African American, Evan had grown up fairly ignorant of how racism still lurks in American culture and how it shadowed his whole life. Waking up to the bigger picture during his years in college, he was quickly overwhelmed. The invisible hand that was holding his people down seemed too heavy for anyone to lift—even if they knew how. The church that was God's instrument on earth seemed as much a part of the problem as anything else. He could spend himself trying to make a difference, and he did. Not much changed in the world, though. He had to fight to believe that the God who gave personal peace to so many could also bring peace to his whole people.

These people, like so many others, know that they are facing something too big for them. They need help. If all I had was a gospel that said, "Confess you are guilty and God will accept you," I would be crippled as a witness. I would be no help to them and would not be able to show how the glory of the gospel meets these people in their need.

My church has quite a number of folks who have come to us via the twelve-step program. Knowing that they are caught in addiction, they don't need us to tell them they are guilty, that they need help or even that God is the source of the help. They do need the good news that Jesus is the Savior come from God, the only one who can rescue them from evil and all its bleak consequences. A gospel of a mighty Savior can be a powerful proclamation of the good news.

GOD OUR SAVIOR

People have always looked for heroes who can stand up for them. They are the stars of every culture's mythology, the bright spots in our histories. The Hellenistic world of the New Testament was no different. The title "Savior" would conjure up images of a god rescuing the world or of a human leader who defeated the enemy and brought peace. So when the apostles proclaimed Jesus as Savior, their Gentile hearers had a way to connect—here was a great hero to deliver them.

But the apostles themselves were Jewish, and their culture had pictures of the Savior wrought out through their living history. They not only had longings for a deliverer, they had dealt with him. Salvation wasn't a myth, a wish or a promise of civil religion; it was God's work in their midst. The nation of Israel was founded on the salvation of God. The great event of the Exodus was nothing other than a rescue, a mighty act of salvation. Their cultural life had reminders of this salvation woven into its fabric. As Moses said to the Israelites, "In days to come, when your son asks you, 'What does this mean?' say to him, 'With a mighty hand the LORD brought us out of Egypt, out of the land of slavery.' . . . And it will be like a sign on your hand and a symbol on your forehead that the LORD brought us out of Egypt with his mighty hand" (Exodus 13:14,16). That was who they were—a people who existed solely because of the mighty hand of God. They also knew not just that the Lord had fought to bring them up out of Egypt, but that he had also established them in the Promised Land: "It was not by their sword that they won the land, nor did their arm bring them victory; it was your right hand, your arm, and the light of your face, for you loved them" (Psalm 44:3).

So they knew they had a savior. When life was hard for them, they returned to their Savior God and asked him to work for them as he had in those days. And the faithful kept that expectation alive right up to the time of Jesus. Listen to the songs in Luke: Mary sings, "My spirit rejoices in God my Savior. . . . He has performed mighty deeds with his arm. . . . He has helped his servant Israel, remembering to be merciful to Abraham and his descendents forever" (1:47, 51, 54-55). Zechariah sings of Jesus as "salvation from our enemies" (1:71), and Simeon says, "My eyes have seen your salvation . . . a light for revelation to the Gentiles and for glory to your people Israel" (2:30, 32). Jesus walks up out of the Old Testament hope for salvation and himself is the answer to his people's prayers for deliverance.

JESUS AS SAVIOR

Of course, Jesus does not just fit the mold of some earthly idea of a hero or deliverer. The word *savior* is not one that happens to fit him—it was made to describe him. He is the reality; all other saviors, before and after, are likenesses and shadows of him. When he delivers, he doesn't just deal with the current human tools of evil and death, he deals with the great enemies. Paul speaks of him as "our Savior, Christ Jesus, who has destroyed death and has brought life and immortality to light through the gospel" (2 Timothy 1:10).

In Colossians, Paul pictures the cross as this hero's victory:

He forgave us all our sins, having canceled the written code, with its regulations, that was against us and that stood opposed to us; he took it away, nailing it to the cross. And having disarmed the powers and authorities, he made a public spectacle of them, triumphing over them by the cross. (2:13-15)

We'll come back to this puzzling verse later, but for now it's enough to note that Christ is pictured as winning a great battle on our behalf, saving us from the accusation of the law and dominion of the evil spiritual powers that were against us. So this Savior rescues us from the power of the law, the forces of evil and even death.

BINDING THE STRONG MAN

Paul saw Jesus disarming "the powers." Jesus painted an even more concrete picture of his victory over Satan: "No one can enter a strong man's house and carry off his possessions unless he first ties up the strong man. Then he can rob his house" (Mark 3:27). What possessions of Satan would Jesus want to carry off? In the context that Jesus speaks, it is those possessed by demons. Jesus has tied up Satan so he can enter his house and rescue the captives.

I spoke before of Carol, the girl who was being pressured by (let's just say it) demons. In desperation she prayed and was quickly granted angelic guards that she could sometimes see. A God *that* real she could trust, and she ran to the cross of that Savior in a hurry. As her progress in the faith became surer, her heart stronger in itself and less vulnerable, the visible spiritual battle faded into the background. But, like the Israelites, she will never forget the tangible salvation she experienced. And the memory helps her stand firm as she faces new challenges as the years go by.

Sometimes the powers of evil are subtle, and sometimes they are not. Either way, the gospel image reassures us by clearly saying, "You, dear children, are from God and have overcome them, because the one who is in you is greater than the one who is in the world" (1 John 4:4).

JESUS ON THE MARCH

Jesus saves us from everything that would bind us and even from our

most destructive enemies. Bernard of Clairvaux (1090-1153) saw Jesus
on a campaign against sin and death: "You have two enemies, sin and
death; that is to say, the death of the body and the death of the soul. He
comes to conquer both, and will save you from both."[1]

Stage one of the campaign was to establish a beachhead, a sin-free
zone from which to launch his attack. That beachhead was his own
body: "He has already overcome sin in his own person by taking a human nature without any blemish: so do not be afraid. Great violence was
done to sin and it is known to have been defeated when nature (of which
it was boasting that it had entirely infected and possessed it) was found
completely free from it in Christ."[2]

Having made himself a strong base, Jesus moves out: "From now on
He pursues your enemies and catches them and does not turn back until
they are defeated. His whole way of life is a fight against sin. He fights it
by both word and example; in His passion He binds it, and overcomes
it, and plunders its spoils."[3]

Bernard pictures Jesus fighting death in the same manner, in stages
from his birth to the end of the age. "He overcomes death also by similar
stages, first in Himself, in His resurrection as the first fruits of them that
sleep and the first-born from among the dead. He will fight death later
on in all of us also, when he will raise up our mortal bodies and destroy
this our last enemy."[4] Jesus is on the move, and even our fiercest enemies
are history.

WAITING IN HOPE

This salvation, like all the images of the gospel, shows the reality of God's
work as being started now and also as awaiting completion on that last
day. Like the Israelites, we have been brought up out of slavery but are
not yet secure in the Promised Land. Or to use the picture of Scottish
preacher and writer George MacDonald, "A man's heart may leap for joy
the moment when, amidst the sea-waves, a strong hand has laid hold of
the hair of his head; he may cry aloud, 'I am saved;'-and he may be safe,
but he is not saved; this is far from a salvation to suffice."[5]

But the day is coming when our rescue will be complete: "Our citizenship is in heaven. And we eagerly await a Savior from there, the Lord Jesus Christ, who, by the power that enables him to bring everything under his control, will transform our lowly bodies so that they will be like his glorious body" (Philippians 3:20-21).

We are saved in Jesus—saved enough to look forward eagerly to our salvation coming in its fullness.

MORE THAN ABLE

After Paul gives that picture of the awaited Savior in Philippians, he shows what holding that picture does for us: "Therefore, my brothers, you whom I love and long for, my joy and crown, that is how you should stand firm in the Lord, dear friends!" (Philippians 4:1). Paul is in jail, his enemies are stirring up trouble for him, others are trying to lead his people astray, and his life itself is on the line—but he knows a mighty Savior is on his side.

When you are guilty, the power of a great Judge is an ominous thing. When you are oppressed, the power of a Rescuer who loves you is a great comfort and encouragement. His power is power *for* you, against all comers. Do we know those who are burdened by poverty, mental illness, spiritual attack? Do we see people in the grip of addictions, compulsions, habits they can no longer control? Do we speak to those who are living under a terrible boss, who are dealing with a corrupt official or who are struggling to raise a family in a poisonous culture? We have a word of hope for all of them. We are not offering an opiate for these masses, but a strong Warrior on the side of the powerless, one who will fight for them until they are free.

My friend Evan is still angry about the burden his fellow African Americans live under. But he takes comfort knowing that their Savior is angry too. Evan has no need for vengeance; he just wants deliverance. For him, waiting for the Lord is hard work, often harder than the work of laboring with the Lord. But he still perseveres in both and still can count his citizenship in heaven. He awaits a Savior from there to work in power down here. And to still be waiting is a victory of faithfulness.

SPEAK TENDERLY

A savior has come, and will come. This word of good news comes to the
people with compassion: "Speak tenderly to Jerusalem. . . . See, the Sov-
ereign LORD comes with power. . . . He tends his flock like a shepherd"
(Isaiah 40:2, 10-11). He comes in power from heaven, his sword drawn,
to protect and comfort his people. This is how Jesus comes: "When he
saw the crowds, he had compassion on them, because they were harassed and helpless, like sheep without a shepherd" (Matthew 9:36). In
this image of the gospel, we are seeing God deal with the evil that is
against his people, the evil that oppresses them from outside themselves.
It pictures us not as doers of evil but as victims and prisoners of evil.

Some of us might be more comfortable with gospel-talk that focuses
on people as evildoers. But we must be fluent in all the languages of the
gospel, so that we can be ready to speak to whomever God brings to us.
This image gives us language that lets us take in the wounded, the harassed and the oppressed.

We need to be capable of seeing situations though the lens that this
image gives us. One woman I know came to her church as a teenager
asking for help. Her father, a church member, was sexually abusing her.
What she heard from them was "Repent of your anger. Submit to your
parents." They also told her father to repent, but took no other action.
The abuse didn't stop, our friend received no comfort, and to this day
she believes the gospel only with the greatest trouble.

No human situation is simple, and there was a lot going on in this
story. But do you see here a church that was able to see and speak only
one side of the gospel? All that church could see was people who should
be told to stop sinning. Their job was to speak to sinners, and they believed that the benefits of the gospel would come when the sinners
stepped into line. But what if they also had trained their hearts to see
God's harassed and helpless people? What if they had known that the
cross showed God's heart to gather up and comfort the wounded? What

if they saw him as having the power to intervene to save a powerless child—and her whole family?

We must let each image of the gospel teach us its lessons. This language of salvation lets us see people not only as perpetrators but also as victims, as the sinned-against as well as the sinners. This is a true way to see, and we must be able to do it in order to wisely bring the power of the gospel to the lives of people around us.

MERELY VICTIMS?

Are we now seeing people no longer as sinners but merely as innocent victims? Victims surely, but not really innocent. The other images of the gospel have been quite clear not only that we *have* a problem, but that we also *are* the problem. But we don't even have to leave the realm of this salvation image to see that we are not merely innocent victims.

The New Testament says we are saved from many things, including disaster on the day of judgment: "For God did not appoint us to suffer wrath but to receive salvation through our Lord Jesus Christ" (1 Thessalonians 5:9). And, of course, who executes that dreaded judgment but God himself? So it is God's just wrath we are saved from:

> Since we have now been justified by his blood, how much more shall we be saved from God's wrath through him! For if, when we were God's enemies, we were reconciled to him through the death of his Son, how much more, having been reconciled, shall we be saved through his life! (Romans 5:9-10)

The Savior God needs to save us from . . . himself? Well, yes. We've embraced the object of his wrath, and we will share in its destruction unless he rescues us out of that entanglement. And entanglement it is, one that we can't get out of. Our choices lead us into sin, but we can't simply choose to come out. Our relationship to sin is something like the relationship of alcoholics to their drink. At one point they chose it freely, but after a number of free choices, the situation is very different. They are under the power of what they had chosen, and they are not free to merely choose out of that state. Like the alcoholic, we find that something we took hold of now has hold of us. In choosing it, we lost the power of choice. We are now trapped.

This is how Paul talks of the plight of the sinner in Romans 7: "I am unspiritual, sold as a slave to sin. . . . The evil I do not want to do—this I keep on doing. Now if I do what I do not want to do, it is no longer I who do it, but it is sin living in me that does it." Paul's best, true self sees his entanglement with sin and hates it. So his sin is really an alien power, but it is also his. He is responsible for this evil he is wrapped up in but can't escape. "What a wretched man I am!" Truly. But our God is a savior who can even do the delicate soul-surgery needed to separate us from our sin: "Who will rescue me from this body of death? Thanks be to God—through Jesus Christ our Lord!"

Jesus can rescue us even from our own choices. I promised to come back to Colossians 2:13-15, and now is a good time. One of the troubling things about that passage is how it talks about the law, God's law, as something we need to be saved from. He actually "cancelled the written code, with its regulations, that was against us and that stood opposed to us; he took it away, nailing it to the cross" (v. 14). God's good law became a force against us when we had done wrong. And it seems that our rebellion against God armed the powers against us, gave them some hold over us. By liberating us from our entanglement with evil, Jesus whisks us away from the impending judgment by the law, strips the demonic powers of the world of any tool they could use against us and pulls us off our self-chosen road toward hell.

So again, we are victims but not innocent. We created our sins, and then they took on a life of their own and threatened to undo us.

Ellen, the woman who was terrified by who she was becoming, was answered by her Savior. Though she had the privilege of studying in Europe and had no material wants, her heart was getting darker by the day. She thought over and over about her friend who had committed suicide, of her own bouts with depression and of her lack of any real vision for her life. She had given into the bitterness and soon stepped willingly into a destructive relationship. Then she looked into her soul one day and saw that she was on a slippery slope, headed down into darkness. So she called out to God.

"Oh God, help!" That simple prayer was what first burst out of her. God needs no explanations, no cajoling. In Jesus, he has already shown that he will pay the greatest price to save us, that he waits on high for this very prayer and that he is by our side the moment we even whisper, "Oh God, help."

God was there in a moment, but he had to lead her out of her bondage step by step, as he did with his people when he brought them up from Egypt. There were no quick miracles for Ellen, just a steady presence and guidance as she climbed back into faith. She has had struggles since, and relying on God is hard. But she has no desire to descend into the pit of bitterness again, and her Lord has the strength to make sure it won't happen.

We need to be saved from many things, including what we ourselves have done. And so the words given to Joseph are true, "You are to give him the name Jesus, because he will save his people from their sins" (Matthew 1:21).

SAVED FROM OUR SINS

So does this mean that whenever people are victims, it's their fault? Well, that might be true if each human being lived in his or her own little universe. But we actually live together as a race, in one world. Entangled with sin and connected to each other, we sin and are sinned against continually, spread out across the planet like a huge dysfunctional family.

So when we pray, "Save us from our sins," we can mean quite a few things. Of course it can mean "save *me* from *my* sins." But it often also means "save me from *their* sins." This was the cry of many psalmists as they faced personal enemies, and it was the cry of the Israelites as they lived under the oppression of the Egyptians.

His salvation also works even closer to home. When we learn our terrible part in the human story, we can, like Paul, lament the ruin that our sins bring on us. But we can also see our sin and cry out that others be saved from it: "God, save *them* from *my* sins." As a father I know this prayer too well. I have known the Savior since before I had children, but I have not been completely disentangled from my sin yet. (Truth be told, part of my sin is that I have not always been very willing to be rescued from it.) I can see too many ways that the evil still in me hurts the people in my life, especially my family. So often I cry out, "Oh God, don't let me hold them back." Some nights I can go to sleep only because I know he is a deliverer.

As we sin together, we might also cry out together. When our churches see how we might cause seekers to stumble, or when our nation does not live up to its ideals, we can pray, "God, save them from our sins!" (Of course, part of his answer may be to work on us so that we sin less. Amen, let him deliver us then!)

We, the human family, have loosed these things on ourselves as we have rebelled from God. Now they are out of our control; they have grown into unstoppable habits, unjust institutions, open doors for Satan. Individuals wound each other in the struggle to survive. Whole peoples are downtrodden because of greed and fear. We sin and are sinned against at every level. What a wretched people we are! Who will save us from this society of death? We have no other hope but the one who came to save his people from their sins.

THE PRICE IS ADMISSION

I was recently in a church worship service, singing "Amazing Grace," and noticed the words had been changed. "Amazing grace, how sweet the sound that saved a wretch like me!" had become "Amazing grace, how sweet the sound that saved *someone* like me." I can only imagine that someone thought *wretch* was too strong a word, one that might put people off. *Wretches? Slaves?* These *are* strong words. I do want help, but I hate admitting that I'm in as bad a shape as all that. Perhaps I don't need rescue really, maybe just a hand here and there. Though this picture of wretchedness is part of a wonderful image of good news, it takes a lot to step in and take my place in it.

This image has a demanding beauty. The demand is that we admit that we need help. Some people are quite ready and will have made this admission years before we have ever met them. Others will choke on the very thought. I admit that I'll give it lip service and then turn around the next moment and act as if that very admission proved what a decent Christian I am after all. If the admission is tough to make, it's even harder to maintain. But every true speaking of the gospel carries a call to us. The way this image speaks repentance and belief is "Call out to the Savior, and wait for him."

Repentance is a turning, and to call out to a savior you need to turn to him. The first thing you must admit is that you cannot handle the situation; you don't have the resources in yourself to cope. This is hard, but many do make that step. They have turned from an unhealthy self-reliance. But we must also turn to the right savior.

We are very good at looking for salvation, really. We do it all the time: I am lonely; that special someone will make my life wonderful. The world is a scary place; money will protect me. My country is a mess; the revolution will bring a new age. I am getting older, but I've got my health club, a facelift, some vitamin C . . .

This salvation of Jesus calls us away from all other ways of salvation. These things may be good in themselves, but we must reject them as strategies that will give us life and freedom. This is a struggle for many believers, to keep believing and acting as if Jesus was our one true Savior. Because we are in the middle of the story, our final salvation is something we still wait for. So it is tempting to reach for other, more available means of salvation. But the call of the gospel is to "wait on the Lord."

MORE DYNAMIC IN OUR DELIVERANCE

This image of the gospel is so powerful, and so needed, why does most of the American church ignore it? Are we so secure in ourselves that we don't really need a savior? If we could admit Jesus as Savior more into our life, thought and witness, we would have a lot of freedom and joy. The people of Dynamic Deliverance have a precious treasure of the gospel in their midst because they can admit it is for them. The more we can enter into this gift, the more we will have to say to many who are, often under the surface, suffering and crying out for deliverance. The gospel will whisper to them, "There is a Savior coming. Just call out and he will come to you." What news could be better?

RANSOM AND REDEMPTION

Love Pays

A woman I know showed up one day at her ex-boyfriend's door—with fresh stitches on both of her wrists. Another called her ex and said he should come find her at her apartment. He did, and found her with a stomach full of sleeping pills.

These women didn't want to die; they wanted to be loved and valued. They were saying, "My life is worth nothing unless you value me. Choose me! Save me! Value me!" Now, they chose an unhealthy form of communication, to be sure. But what they wanted wasn't much different from what we all want and need. We are all thirsty for worth, to be considered valuable.

The images of ransom and redemption show how the gospel meets this need. They have a lot in common with the image of salvation, but their focus is different and they add something new. These images show that the rescue out of bondage was done at a price. Just how far God was willing to go to save us shows what we mean to him.

THE PAYMENT THAT FREES

The New Testament writers chose language that brought this out. *Ransom* meant something close to what we mean by it today. While we usually think of it connected with a kidnapping, hearers in that world would have thought immediately of prisoners of war. When an army would capture enemy troops, they would take note of any noble or high-ranking people they had captured. They would then offer to give them back to their own people, if their people valued them enough to pay the price. Of course, most of the prisoners wouldn't be ransomed; they would be left as slaves—their countries in general didn't care enough, and the few who did couldn't pay. But some happy few were freed.

The word *redemption* could be used this way, but it could also mean the price that buys a slave out of slavery. The owner was paid, either by the slave or by someone else, whatever the slave was worth to the owner. The slave was then free and could never be brought back into slavery.

These would be clear images for those first hearers of the gospel. As New Testament scholar Leon Morris says, "Redemption was part of the language of ordinary people in their ordinary everyday life. Christians could use it knowing it was a vivid picture-word, a word which everyone could understand and which, properly used, conveyed forcefully one important aspect of Christian teaching."[1]

This was all from the first-century context. Of course, to the Jewish apostles, ransom and redemption had a very familiar, Old Testament ring. The great redemption was the rescue out of Egypt. And smaller redemptions happened all the time. In the sacrificial system, every firstborn animal belonged to God, but you could sometimes redeem it with another animal or a certain amount of money. In economic life, if you went broke and had to sell your property—or even yourself—a kinsman-redeemer could come and buy it—or you—back. Like the idea of ransoming prisoners, redemption wasn't just a rescue or just a purchase; it was deliverance at a price.

THE RIGHT PRICE

With the idea of price so firmly rooted in the word, here comes an interesting problem. The great redemption of Israel, the liberation from the bondage of slavery in Egypt, didn't involve money or even an exchange. God didn't seem to pay anything to anyone; he just brought the people up out of Egypt with his "mighty hand and an outstretched arm" (Deuteronomy 4:34). But he did "stretch forth" that arm. Jewish and Christian commentators have often taken this to mean that the effort God exerted was the redemption price. What it took him to do the job was the price he paid.

"So God didn't *really* pay then." I am tempted to think this because I naturally think that money is the *real* way to pay for something. A little extra work is often what I am willing to do to get out of paying the full price for something. But it turns out that I have been trained to value money too highly. Work is the real, or natural, price to pay for anything worth having.

Think for a moment about how you pay for your food: Most of us go to the supermarket, pay our money and take our food home. But how does the farmer pay for his food? When he sits down at his table, he is receiving what he truly paid for out of his own self. He paid in sweat and toil, early mornings and late nights, careful planning and backbreaking work. This is the "price" that bought life from the dust of the earth. My money seems a poor stand-in compared with this.

Now, I am not against money; I'm not proposing a return to a barter economy. What I take from all this is simply the reminder that money is an artificial way to pay for what you get. It is not a living and natural price. The sweat of the worker is a more honest, more intrinsic way to pay for what is produced. So when God pays for the Israelites with his own effort, it is a deeper and more meaningful payment than if he handed over something outside himself. There is no medium of exchange in this redemption; he offers up his own sweat and toil for his people's release.

But did the omnipotent God of the universe break a sweat in overcoming the ancient Egyptians? How much did it really take out of him? The answer is certainly more complicated than it seems, and it would do us no harm to ponder it.[2] But we can set that meditation aside for now. The picture of God's redemption becomes sharp and clear as we move on to look at Jesus. In Jesus, we see the deep redemption of which the Exodus was only a shadow. And the price of that saving effort can be seen clearly, for God's saving arm is Jesus.

PAYING IN SWEAT AND BLOOD

In Jesus we see God paying for us in sweat and blood:

> During the days of Jesus' life on earth, he offered up prayers and
> petitions with loud cries and tears to the one who could save him
> from death, and he was heard because of his reverent submission.
> Although he was a son, he learned obedience from what he suf-
> fered and, once made perfect, he became the source of eternal sal-
> vation for all who obey him. (Hebrews 5:7-9)

Coming to his fallen people and living faithfully among them carried
a price. The capstone of that life was the cross, where the price became
nothing less than himself, "for the Son of Man did not come to be served,
but to serve, and to give his life as a ransom for many" (Mark 10:45).

The people he loved were caught in bondage to an "empty way of
life," trapped in "wickedness" and caught under the "curse of the law" (1
Peter 1:18; Titus 2:14; Galatians 3:13). But he poured out his life in the
work of freeing them: "You are worthy . . . because you were slain, and
with your blood you purchased for God members of every tribe and language and people and nation" (Revelation 5:9 TNIV).

If the cry of our heart is "Value me!" God answers us beyond our wild-
est hopes. He says, "Here's how I value you: I will give my own Son for
you."

A GOOD PRICE?

Christians are used to hearing this, and we should come back to it often.
But hearing it often without hearing it afresh can dull us. We can miss
its potential impact on our own hearts and on those around us. Some are
drawn powerfully to this sacrifice, and others are repelled.

This world is a dark place where people are often made to suffer for
the gain of others, but not because they choose to. Students of Western
imperialism and slavery see the cross used this way, and yes, it has been
used to say, "Be good and accept suffering," while the masters prosper.
Many people also see God as a cold judge demanding that Jesus fulfill

his mission and die, even though Jesus asked that he might not. God's mercy seems to come at his Son's expense. Who is going to trust a father who hands his own son over to die?

We have to let Jesus speak clearly to them. He values us and agrees to the price he pays. When he talks of himself as the good Shepherd he says,

> "I lay down my life for the sheep. . . . The reason my Father loves me is that I lay down my life—only to take it up again. No one takes it from me, but I lay it down of my own accord. I have authority to lay it down and authority to take it up again. This command I received from my Father." (John 10:15, 17-18)

The Father, Son and Spirit are in beautiful agreement about what you are worth. The Lord of the universe, the source of all life and love and goodness, thought you worth dying for.

SEEING THE VALUE

Is this guy really worth it? Late at night, looking at Pamela's friend, Bill, I wondered. My wife and I had been over at Pamela's, talking late at night, when she got the phone call. Bill was calling for help—from the local police station. So down we went.

Pamela is a kind, helpful person with lots of friends, including many I hadn't met. Bill was one of those, and I wasn't impressed. He looked contrite enough, but his story made him look pretty stupid. He had run a red light, and when a cop tried to pull him over, he'd run. Now he had called Pamela to bail him out.

As she paid the bail, I had a hard time thinking he was worth it. Was he just taking advantage of her kindness? Did he plan to shape up after this? Or was this just a waste of her time and money—and care?

I look over my church and often catch myself in the same thoughts. Our church has communion every week, and I tend to sit for a while and watch as the lines of people go down for the bread and the cup. There at the tables are the symbols of what Christ paid for them, his own body and blood. And there, going down to receive these gifts, are ordinary people I often discount. Some of the people are good looking, some not. Some I like, some I don't. Young and old, fit and lumpy, deep and shallow, they are all welcomed to celebrate and accept the price Jesus paid for them. And I am invited to drop my judgments of them and judge them as he does, as people of infinite worth.

So I smile ruefully at being caught once again at being such a judgmental pig, then get up and get in line with everyone else. When you see this arrogant man in the line, sisters and brothers, look on him and love him. Jesus paid a lot to get him in the door, and soon it will be obvious what he's worth. But until then, just trust that Jesus knew what he was doing when he bought him at such a price.

A FUTURE BOUGHT AND PAID FOR

Our value isn't obvious yet; the redemption isn't yet complete. Like every other image we have seen, these images of ransom and redemption look both backward and forward. In Ephesians we hear that in Christ "we have redemption through his blood, the forgiveness of sins, in accordance with the riches of God's grace" (1:7). Here we are surely looking at the done deal, what was definitively done for us in the death of Jesus. But, in almost the next breath, he is telling us that the Spirit in us "is a deposit guaranteeing our inheritance until the redemption of those who are God's possession" (1:14).

We are already "God's possession," yet we wait for our redemption. It recalls Israel's place, when God was in the middle of redeeming them from bondage. He had shown up, worked in power and declared they were his: "Let *my* people go." The job was as good as done, and only the hard of heart couldn't see it. But the people had not yet been completely extricated from that bondage, and they still had to look forward to the inheritance of their own land. They had to wait and watch, follow and trust.

Paul, who is so firm on the reality of what God has already done for us, is also certain that we are still waiting in hope: "We ourselves, who have the firstfruits of the Spirit, groan inwardly as we wait eagerly for our adoption as sons, the redemption of our bodies." (Romans 8:23) The redemption of God goes deep down into our souls and deals with unseen realities, but it won't be invisible forever. A "day of redemption" is coming (Ephesians 4:30). Then not only our bodies but the whole physical universe "will be liberated from its bondage to decay and brought into the glorious freedom of the children of God" (Romans 8:21).

So that is the picture of ransom and redemption: a great price has been paid for us. We can live knowing that God considers us worth everything to him: "He who did not spare his own Son, but gave him up for us all—how will he not also, along with him, graciously give us all things?" (Romans 8:32). As we wait, we can be sure that he will take care of us—and bring us all the way home.

The great value he places on us calls for response. It calls us to come to him and to stay with him.

WHO LOVES YOU LIKE I DO?

"I love you so much." "I love you more than life itself." "Forever I am yours." Love always says things like this. Half of all the music on the radio is songs talking grandly of the singer's love for the sung-to. The other half is songs of broken-heartedness, because the promises weren't kept. There are shining exceptions, glimpses of real love in the world, but mostly there is talk of love. And talk really is cheap.

But one man doesn't just put his money where his mouth is; he puts his life there: "But God demonstrates his own love for us in this: While we were still sinners, Christ died for us" (Romans 5:8). Love not just spoken but demonstrated—nothing is more powerful.

Charissa was a Christian woman who had just begun to follow Jesus. Newly in love with Jesus, she tried to be a witness to her nominally Jewish roommate, Monica. On and off through the year she had tried to tell Monica how much Jesus meant to her and how he had changed her life, but to Monica it sounded like standard love-song fare from someone newly infatuated with religion.

But one day, on a long walk, Monica was ready, and Charissa was able to put together the story in a way Monica could grasp. She had always known about God, but he seemed far-off and rather vague. On that walk, however, she got a picture of who Charissa had been "singing" of all along. "All of a sudden God had a face," Monica said later, "and then he went and died for me. How could I not love him back?"

Charissa wasn't well versed in the ancient context for redemption or in the myriad passages about what Christ had done; she just knew the basics: God loves us, Christ died for us, and that changes everything. What more do we really need?

DON'T GO BACK

Any love can fade after that first encounter; human hearts are just not as constant as God's. And the love of God can seem so distant, the demonstration of his love like a page from an ancient history book. But we live here and now, and it is tempting not to remember, not to wait and to reach out for value now, close at hand.

"My friends weren't even calling me to go out anymore, since I became a Christian. I just went out to show them I could still have fun."

"I know this relationship probably won't be great for my faith, but— it's so great!"

"Look, I'm not selling my soul. . . . At work you just do what you have to; you just get by."

Even the message "I have loved you with my life" comes with a call to repent and believe. The price paid for us has a demanding beauty of its own. We have to turn away from bent, unhealthy and cheapening attempts at being valued. All the games that are played in the world are out-of-bounds for us. Peter calls them empty: "For you know that it was not with perishable things such as silver or gold that you were redeemed from the empty way of life handed down to you from your forefathers, but with the precious blood of Christ, a lamb without blemish or defect" (1 Peter 1:18-19).

As brothers and sisters, we have to be like Peter and preach the gospel to one another. We have to talk sense into each other. Once, at a party in my high school days, I managed to get more than a little drunk. I found a female acquaintance in the same state and, having enough brain function left to remember the possibilities of male-female relationships, I headed outside with her. Some of my more sober friends followed us out and stopped us. I have a blurry memory of my friend Jim earnestly telling me not to be stupid: "You are really going to regret this tomorrow, man." His words, and greater sobriety, won the day.

We have to urge each other to hang on and value the precious life that was given for us. If we love each other, we will urge each other not to do things we will regret in the morning. For "our salvation is nearer now than when we first believed. The night is nearly over; the day is almost here" (Romans 13:11-12).

The day of redemption is coming, when the great price paid for us will have its full effect. A people secure in the love of God, freed from the entanglements of sin and waiting patiently to be claimed by their Savior can be an island of sanity and a beacon of hope in the world. All we have to do is believe our own gospel.

FREEDOM

Free for Life

Jesus came to a synagogue of respectable people and said he had come to "proclaim freedom for the prisoners" (Luke 4:18). Did he mean *them?* Later he stood in front of an average crowd of people and said, "I tell you the truth, everyone who sins is a slave to sin. . . . If the Son sets you free, you will be free indeed" (John 8:34, 36). And they said, "Slaves? We're not slaves."

In our world there are too many people who are literally slaves and prisoners. The 2006 UNICEF report speaks of 8.4 million children "working under horrific circumstances." About 1.8 million children are trapped in prostitution and the pornography industry, 5.7 million in forced and bonded labor. Hundreds of thousands are pressed into the service of militias around the world. God sees this and has sent his people to go out and work with him for their freedom.[1]

But in our "free" society, as in that crowd around Jesus, there is also bondage—far more slavery than meets the eye.

UNSEEN SLAVERY

On the college campuses I visit, I constantly meet bright, successful students—who are slaves. Academic success and careerism promise the moon, but end up being harsh masters. Of course, one might just be working hard for the joy of it or for the admirable goal of doing good work in the world. But I remember one young man who gave himself away quite clearly.

He gave his schoolwork the highest priority and allowed no other commitment to jeopardize the completion of any assignment. He seemed to be in control of his academics, but I wondered if they were in control of him. So I had suggested to him that he take a Sabbath, obeying God's rule of a holy day off. His eyes widened, there was a sharp intake of breath, and I knew what I was seeing even before he opened his mouth. It was the fight-or-flight response, the reaction of a creature sensing danger. I knew then that his work was not a joy he pursued but a monster he kept at bay. He was a slave, toiling after a dream of success while pursued by the specter of failure. Before his rationality engaged and came to his defense, the reality of his slavery had shown on his face.

"Each one is tempted when, by his own evil desire, he is dragged away and enticed" (James 1:14) When our desires are not put before God, we are dragged around by anyone who promises to fulfill them. We desire success and end up enslaved to our work. We dance at the end of the advertiser's strings, chasing after pleasure, success, good looks, youth— the good life. Promised freedom, we find only the unending slavery of consumerism. And how many people these days will submit themselves to a cosmetic surgeon's knife because that harsh master—our cult of beauty—demands it?

FIGHTING FOR FREEDOM

Sometimes we fight back, we struggle against all kinds of oppression for ourselves and for the sake of others. I was impressed a few years ago when actress Jamie Lee Curtis struck a blow against the Hollywood image machine. It was an exposé of sorts, appearing in *More:* Ms. Curtis posed without makeup in a sports bra and spandex briefs.[2] Side by side with this was a glamour shot, showing how makeup, clothing and photographic tricks can project unreal images of the stars. The point was that we've been lied to. No one can look as good as the stars—not even the stars. These images, which create unreachable ideals that oppress girls and women by the millions, are fakes.

I rejoiced at Curtis's courage to expose the lie. As a husband and a father of three teenage daughters, I have come to hate the weight that the cult of appearance places on the backs of women. Body-image bondage sends far too many women into eating disorders, needless cosmetic surgery and frantic lives of trying to measure up. I was glad to see someone fight back.

A few people I knew mentioned the article. Perhaps some people here and there had a key moment of realization. But the image machine rumbles on, spewing out its lies about who women are and who they should be. The oppression continues.

FREE INDEED

We are burdened with all kinds of bondage, and often we struggle against it. But we can't seem to find lasting freedom. To this world Jesus comes with a promise of real freedom: "If the Son sets you free, you will be free indeed" (John 8:36). This image of freedom is in many ways like the image of salvation we have already seen, but it carries a different emphasis or feel. Freedom is not only a negative thing: freedom *from* this or that. It is also positive: freedom *for* living. In this section we are looking at being delivered *from* external forces, but the imagery of freedom also speaks of what we were saved *for*. In this way freedom as an image sits on the cusp and could easily wrap back around to our beginning and the image of life. Freedom does have that same thrill of promise, of vital energy, that images of life have.

Only the gospel has the power to give real and lasting freedom. But in our culture, Christianity is not famous for giving freedom. Our religion is famous for saying *No!* Repression, rather than freedom, is our reputation. How can a gospel of freedom come from the people who brought you Puritans? Christianity does say no often, but slavery is what it says no to, so that we can say a resounding yes to God.

SLAVES TO RIGHTEOUSNESS

Paul tries to make this clear as he makes his case in Romans 6. He has gone along in Romans using different images of salvation, and here he picks up the pictures of slavery and freedom. He talks of baptism, picturing our union with the death and life of Jesus: "If we have been united with him like this in his death, we will certainly also be united with him in his resurrection" (Romans 6:5). Being united with his death means we are "no longer slaves to sin—because anyone who has died has been freed from sin."

This is sounding good so far. We are free, "for sin shall not be your master, because you are not under law, but under grace" (Romans 6:14). We have died to sin; twisted, evil desires are no longer our master. So what kind of life do we have now that we are free? "You have been set free from sin and have become slaves to righteousness" (6:18). Slaves again! This is just what so many people fear from God—that he will be just another harsh master.

I have said that the gospel speaks of what we have been saved from and what we have been saved for. In the image of freedom, it is clear that slavery is what we are saved from. And there seems to be a promise of freedom: "It is for freedom that Christ has set us free" (Galatians 5:1). But what can Paul mean that we are saved *for* a slavery, a slavery to righteousness?

Paul gives his reasons for this language in the next breath: "I put this in human terms because you are weak in your natural selves." The clue is that we are weak in our natural selves. What is weak in us? Our hearts. We don't know anything like the whole-hearted devotion he is talking about. We've never seen anything voluntarily entered into—not even romance—that is close to what he means. It's our love and devotion that are weak in our natural selves; we don't have any idea how to picture the fierce bond to goodness that he wants for us.

So he reaches for a picture of the bond of slavery. This kind of bond, though it is evil, has the permanence and the all-consuming nature he wants to communicate. Seen this way, slavery is a parody, a dark shadow, of devotion and dedication. Paul is looking for a picture of an unbreakable dedication. Perhaps, he reasons, even though our devotions are all weak and impermanent, we will understand the unbreakable bond of slavery. Anyone who has striven for excellence in music or sports knows that this devotion can look like slavery. But in this beautiful reality of dedication, the regimens, the work and the pain are entered into freely. For the love of the game or the desire for excellence, we voluntarily put ourselves under harsh taskmasters—our teachers, our coaches.

A REGIMEN FOR LIFE

When my daughters were in gymnastics, they would happily rush into a big room where adults would make them run around and do pushups, stretches and stomach crunches. There was something there, in all the work, that drew them and made it good.

I saw it as I watched a good teacher work with my daughter Maura's gymnastics class. Julian had a build that said "football player," and he dwarfed the sprightly seven- and eight-year-old girls who bounced around him in sparkly leotards. One routine they did was this: Maura would stand on the trampoline with Julian standing over her; then he would give a huge surging bounce that would launch her over his head. In midair she would stretch out flat, horizontal to the ground. Then he would put out his arms as she came down, and catch her. And she would smile.

Why did Maura do this gleefully? Why did she let this huge man throw her into space and then lie flat? Because she trusted that he was not just over her but *for* her. That was how he used his physical power with her, and it is also how he used his orders and his authority. He was teaching his girls to fly.

All those coaches work their girls hard. There are killer stretches and strength exercises, repetitions of the same flips over and over. But they are not doing this for the joy of seeing children follow their orders. They have power, strength and skill that they are trying to pass on to their young charges. They are not satisfied just to show the children good gymnastics or to have the students merely know the terms. They want the abilities worked into the minds and bodies—into the lives—of these kids. They want the girls to have the power and freedom in themselves to leap, tumble, flip and fly.

All those hard disciplines are the way that life, vitality and freedom are worked into students. "You want to be free to vault that horse in good form whenever you need to? Good. Then let's spend the afternoon working on your approach run." Discipline is the path to freedom. The wholehearted binding of the heart to excellence is the path to strong, free life.

That's what all those Christian "things to do" were always meant to be. They are the path to freedom in Christ. Do you want to know "what would Jesus do?" Then study your Bible regularly; learn God's mind. Do you want to be free to love your enemies in a crisis? Practice loving that annoying brother of yours today, and tomorrow. Do you want to say yes to wisdom, clarity and self-control? Say no to the fog of chemical abuse, consumerism and lust.

Jesus is not a teacher who is just keeping us in line; he is one who wants us to have the strength and flexibility of heart, the will power and the endurance we need to live the good life. He is strong among us, but his strength is not for dominating us. His great strength is given to us for our freedom. He brings the unlimited wisdom of the Father in devising our training plan. He uses his freedom to be in all places, to be right there with us during our trials and competitions, to warn and encourage us. He uses his great strength to "spot" us through all that is too difficult for us. He is about freedom, so we can be too. He is free for us, so we can live freely for him.

And Jesus is closer than any coach. Remember, our lives are united to his, so the freedom we get is his very own freedom. Here is a telling question for our faith: Is God about freedom or about control? We will probably not believe that his plan for us is freedom and joy if this is not what we think his own life is like. Coaches and teachers pass on what they have. If God is about power and control, if he is at heart a taskmaster, we can't trust him. Does God have freedom to pass on to us? Can the gospel of freedom be true? Is freedom what he is about?

THE FREEDOM OF GOD

Some kinds of God-talk can make us wonder if God is more of a controller than a liberator. A traditional way of talking about God's power has been to emphasize each thing he has *power over:* he is omniscient (all knowing), omnipresent (in all places at once), omnipotent (capable of doing all things). But we can also speak about all of this power as simply the freedom of God. He is not just *free from* this or that but *free for* being the good God that he is. Is there any lack of knowledge that could keep him from doing the good he wants to do to his creation? No. Is there any way distance separates him from the world he loves? No. Is there any situation in which he would want to do the best, wisest thing and yet be unable? No. He is free to work out all the goodness his character leads him to do.

It goes even deeper. This freedom is not only the way he lives with his creation; it is the way he lives period. We say God is holy, free from evil. He cannot lie, do wrong or even *want* to do wrong. Then we say, "He is not really free then; there is so much he cannot do or even want to do." This is not a limitation, but rather it is his freedom to be himself. Nothing will ever enslave him or make him be less than he can be. To tell someone that they must always be themselves, must always be true to who they are, is to tell them they are free forever. God is free forever to be his good self.

Think of the joy that little children feel in singing or in running through a field. They aren't hemmed in by thoughts of how people will see them. They just do it; they run because they can and because it is good. This is just a shadow of the freedom and joy God feels in living.

A thoughtful Christian friend of mine read these last few sentences and said, "That's strange. I just never thought before whether God had joy like that—that he might enjoy being alive."

Can you imagine it? Are we the only ones who can walk out into the sunlight, breathe deeply of fresh air and say, "It's good to be alive!"? When God saw his creation and said, "It is very good," did he say it in a bored tone? With objective dryness? Can you imagine him exclaiming it with satisfaction, delight or even exuberant joy? Even now he watches each atom, each flower, each supernova, each mother with child. Can you not imagine him rejoicing over every good thing?

God even experiences freedom in his sorrow, grief and anger. Imagine being free from the shadow of evil in yourself. Imagine being sad and knowing it has no trace of foolish self-pity in it. You just know that your sadness is truly for the person you are caring about. Imagine being angry and not being afraid of the hurt your rage might do. You just know that you are angry only at what is truly wrong and that your indignation will only move you to do good. Is there not a purity, a kind of fierce joy here? Can you imagine the freedom of God?

What kind of life do you think God has? Your answer very much determines what you think he's trying to give you. Consider this then: He is alive and he is free. And he is for us. He is not concerned with having power over us, to have us as slaves. His power among us means he is free to give us all his heart desires. What his heart desires, as we have seen in Christ, is to give his life to us. He wants us to grow up into his own fullness and freedom. He wants us to be so fully bound to goodness that an observer with an uncoached heart might call it slavery.

And just think about having that freedom in ourselves. To be told that we must always be ourselves—that we will never be pushed around by fear, never tempted by greed, never slowed down by selfishness, never dragged around by other's opinions, never paralyzed by self-doubt. To know that you can go and be yourself and never look back. These "nevers" are not bondage; they are the freedom that God lives in—the freedom he is giving to us.

FREEDOM FROM FEAR

The gospel shows us a Lord who freely bound himself to us that we might be liberated: "Since the children have flesh and blood, he too shared in their humanity so that by his death he might destroy him who holds the power of death—that is, the devil—and free those who all their lives were held in slavery by their fear of death" (Hebrews 2:14-15).

Held in slavery by the fear of death. This is not just us imagining that one day our hearts will stop beating, as chilling a thought as that can be.

We feel death encroaching daily in many ways, and we frantically push back. We feel we need this or that to survive, and we sacrifice all else in the pursuit of it. We rarely name or face these fears, yet the frightening abyss lives deep in our minds and hearts. And the desperate patterns we develop to protect ourselves we don't name as slavery; we are just "getting by" like everyone else. And it can look so normal.

Susan had always had a boyfriend. Not always the same one, but ever since dating was a thing to do, she did it. It was never very long after one breakup that soon she'd be dating someone else. No one would say that she was desperate; she was just always attached. And if she had to have sex in order to keep a man around, whether she really wanted to or not—well, everyone does it.

She became friends with some Christians in college and became a follower of Jesus. Before long she broke up with her boyfriend . . . and began dating someone in the Christian fellowship. When that relationship went nowhere, she was devastated. Now, though, with some friends around her who knew the gospel, she could see new things about her life and heart. As they talked things through, she realized that she didn't love men (which is wonderful); she needed them to feel fulfilled (which is an addiction). She had a hunger to have a man's touch and approval, and she would do what she needed to get it. But filling that need, living in that slavery, was taking more and more of her life and self. Before she could be in a healthy relationship, she needed to know the freedom of Jesus.

Many older adults love to see young couples walking hand in hand, and that is a fine thing. But through that year I smiled to see a young single woman move through her life without a male companion, learning how to taste the freedom of Jesus.

THE FREEDOM OF JESUS

Jesus died to free us from bondage to fear and to call us to join him in his own freedom. The writer of Hebrews takes chapter eleven to show us many who have become slaves to righteousness, who trusted God and said no to the slaveries of this world so that they might say yes to life with God. Then the writer turns to us with the call to leave behind the fears, sin and slavery that Jesus has already defeated: "Therefore, since we are surrounded by such a great cloud of witnesses, let us throw off everything that hinders and the sin that so easily entangles, and let us run with perseverance the race marked out for us" (Hebrews 12:1). The picture here is so clear: we can shed all the weights and entanglements that keep us from being ourselves, and we can run the race we were born to run.

And it is in his freedom that we run. He himself knows the joy of that fierce bond to goodness: "Let us fix our eyes on Jesus, the author and perfecter of our faith, who for the joy set before him endured the cross, scorning its shame, and sat down at the right hand of the throne of God" (Hebrews 12:2). He endured for us, for our freedom and for his own joy. He knows the true path to freedom, and he takes us with him.

Paul proclaims, "It is for freedom that Christ has set us free. Stand firm, then, and do not let yourselves be burdened again by a yoke of slavery" (Galatians 5:1). Christ set us free, but we need to enter that freedom and stand in it. To do so, we have to accept its demanding beauty.

UNDER THE LASH

Aaron was impressive. Close to straight A's, popular, on the lacrosse team—he even had time to be involved in several clubs. Definitely impressive. The trouble was, he tried hard to be, and it took its toll on him. Hearing from him about his ulcers and mysterious rashes, we talked about the pressure he felt from his family. Whether or not his parents actually sent this message, Aaron felt he had to be everything they never got a chance to be. It was a slavery to someone else's ideal, and it took a harsh toll on him.

The first time his friends brought it up, he vehemently denied anything was wrong. Just like Jesus' hearers who said, "How can you say we are slaves?" Aaron defended his way of life. It was the only one he knew, and the only other option was failure. Admitting that we are slaves is part of the demanding beauty of this gospel image. We need to repent of having devoted our lives to the wrong masters, and that is hard. (Living with those masters, though, is even harder—as Aaron was to find out.)

So he didn't repent and believe then, but his Christian suitemates kept living their lives with him. And when the ulcers got bad, the picture got clearer for Aaron: his way was killing him, and there was a way that gave life. He didn't come around all in one conversation, but he did find his freedom. And I think his parents are happy with the life they see he is now receiving.

A SAFE MASTER

Ellen wasn't going to argue with the gospel's message that the world makes us slaves. Her problem was its call to trust any master at all. Ellen was a spiritual person but was angry at Christianity. For too long it had been a force to repress women; it was anything but a place of freedom. She had Christian friends who she often kept up late in deep discussion. She didn't really consider Jesus, though, till she met Christians who loved her freedom as much as they loved their Jesus. They talked about respect and actually gave it to her. There was a lot she didn't understand, but at least the words and the reality were matching.

Ellen was facing another side of the demanding beauty of this image. We have to *repent,* to admit our slavery, but we also have to *believe,* to trust that God will not be just another harsh master. Trust is hard, one of the hardest things we can do. But to know his freedom we have to come to him. While Ellen still saw many Christians she wouldn't trust as far as she could throw, she did come to see the love in the face of the man Jesus.

Now Ellen has many different Christian friends who have different interpretations of how "the perfect law that gives freedom" (James 1:25) gives its freedom to women. But the beautiful thing she sees is that, arguments aside, when these women live and breathe the gospel, they can find any of those ways as freedom. It's Jesus; he brings it with him wherever he goes. While Ellen still feels free to make the case for her new *Christian* feminism, she is fine with any situation—if Jesus is there.

GO OUT SINGING

Back when we were looking at the image of justification, I pulled out a
Charles Wesley hymn. In the stanza I quoted, he was imagining the great
courtroom scene: "No condemnation now I dread, Jesus and all in him
is mine." Wesley, caught up in the wonder of the gospel, did not stick
with just one gospel image in that hymn, "And Can It Be." He also went
on to sing of his freedom in Christ:

> Long my imprisoned spirit lay, fast-bound in sin and nature's
> night;
> Thine eye diffused a quickening ray, I woke, the dungeon
> flamed with light;
> My chains fell off, my heart was free, I rose, went forth, and fol-
> lowed thee.[3]

We have been given freedom in Jesus; no chains can hold us. You can
look into the coming day and see there the worries, the temptations, the
enemies, the hardships and fears—and know that nothing can hold you
back or rule you. With a free heart you can sing as you walk out with
Jesus.

Can I say it one last time? This is good news.

EPILOGUE

Apples of Gold in Settings of Silver

This short book is only a beginning study. Each chapter skims only the surface of its gospel image, and by no means have I tackled all the images of the New Testament. There are many others to consider: new creation, reconciliation, healing and sanctification, to name a few. The wonders of this gallery will keep us busy for a lifetime, and more.

Even looking at the gospel as a gallery of images has been a little difficult. Every time we find a really good passage on one image, a couple of others are sneaking in the edges or even lurking at its very heart. I wanted to see each one clearly, but we really can't keep them apart; they are distinct but inseparable. Pulling them apart as I did was just an exercise in seeing—and a remedial one at that. Dissecting an animal gives you one kind of knowledge about it, but seeing the living, breathing organism in its natural setting is really the way to know it. The natural setting that we have in the New Testament is encouragement, calling and challenge; it is believers calling each other and the world to come receive life from God. In this setting the images are woven together and called on at need. And the need is the need of the world for God. The gospel is not a subject to be studied or debated; it is a call to be given, a new life to offer. As Moses said of the law, "They are not just idle words for you— they are your life" (Deuteronomy 32:47).

As we explore, speak and live by these truths, they will be our life. We'll begin to have gospel wisdom deep in our hearts, minds and character. Then speaking the gospel will not be a passing on of some outline or seminar (or clever book) but an outflowing of what we really have inside.

Good gospel-speaking, then, comes out of us not like knowledge from the experts but like wisdom from the wise. Proverbs is a good model to take. In Proverbs, wisdom isn't in knowing many things, but in choosing the right truth to apply at the right time. That's why Proverbs is a like a box of gems and not like a computer database. We can't go to the Bible with the right algorithm, the right theology, and crank out the right words to serve the people around us. We must choose the wise response that fits. Proverbs itself tells us how it is to be used—like an expert jeweler fitting stone to setting: "A word aptly spoken is like apples of gold in settings of silver" (Proverbs 25:11).

Knowing the images that express the gospel, and knowing them deeply, we can have the wisdom to speak these words of life "aptly," situating them beautifully in the settings our friends find themselves in. But if we fail to take the wisdom in, we can have fine words that are useless: "Like a lame man's legs that hang limp is a proverb in the mouth of a fool" (Proverbs 26:7).

Gaining deep gospel wisdom may seem like a hard lifelong task, but take heart—it may be hard for everyone, but it is also possible for everyone. Anyone can do it because it is not about cleverness but about wisdom. And "the fear of the LORD is the beginning of wisdom" (Proverbs 9:10); it always comes back to trust and obedience. Knowing Jesus as Lord gives us deep insight into life:

> Oh, how I love your law!
> > I meditate on it all day long.
> Your commands make me wiser than my enemies,
> > for they are ever with me.
> I have more insight than all my teachers,
> > for I meditate on your statutes.
> I have more understanding than the elders,
> > for I obey your precepts. (Psalm 119:97-100)

So there is no cause to worry; this wisdom is available to all. With

Jesus, everyone who asks receives and everyone who searches finds and for everyone who knocks, the door will be opened. So the only question left is, Will you ask? The gospel calls you in, and the door is open.

APPENDIX 1

A Summary of the Images

Summaries always lie. Well, perhaps not, but they can't carry all of the truth, so it is good to be careful with them. That's why I give you the chart on the next pages with a bit of hesitation; I don't want you to imagine that we now have a new gospel presentation that can be neatly packaged. But hand it over I will, because we do need summaries. Our minds can't hold the full truth of anything, and it is better to have clear outlines than fuzzy ones.

So, on the following page is a chart summarizing some of what I have said about these different images and their use. Like notes taken by a good student, these summaries can help you organize the material and help you call it back to mind. Don't let them be a fixed list, an end to your exploration of the gospel, but let them be a beginning, an open door. Study, read, think, find out more about this good news—and tell more.

Some Images of the Gospel

	Image / Vocabulary	The Message	Is good news when . . .	Passages to read
Images of New Life	Life	He has given you what is really life—new, true, abundant and eternal.	Your life seems small or messed up beyond repair. Death feels close.	John 6:35-51; 10:7-10; Mark 8:34-38; Romans 6:1-14; Colossians 3:1-4
	Adoption, Sonship	You are welcomed into God's family.	You are alone, feeling unwanted or unworthy.	Luke 15:11-32; John 1:10-13; Galatians 3:26–4:7; Ephesians 1:3-6; 1 John 2:28–3:10
	Kingdom	You have been called into a new world order.	Life seems too small. You see the world full of evil and injustice.	Mark 1:14-15; Colossians 1:10-14; Matthew 5:1-12; 13:1-52; Philippians 2:5-11
Images of Mercy and Restoration	Justification	You have been declared innocent, approved and right.	You feel guilty. You don't feel good enough to be a Christian.	Luke 18:9-14; Romans 3:19-26; 8:1-4; Galatians 2:11-21; 3:1-14
	Forgiveness	He has wiped out your debt.	You're aware of the damage you've caused and that you can't cover it. You feel like you owe God something.	Matthew 18:21-35; 26:26-29; Mark 2:1-12; Luke 7:36-50; 1 John 1:8-10
	Atonement	He has offered for us the perfect gift to God. He has taken away your sin.	You think your life isn't good enough to be in front of God. You feel shame.	Hebrews 9:11-14; 10:11-14; 1 John 4:7-12; Ephesians 5:1-2; Romans 12:1-2
Images of Deliverance	Salvation	He has rescued you.	You are overcome. You are afraid.	Luke 19:1-10; John 3:16-17; Acts 4:7-12; Colossians 2:13-15; 2 Timothy 1:8-12
	Ransom and Redemption	He bought your freedom at great price.	You are bound. You feel worthless.	Mark 10:42-45; John 10:7-18; Titus 2:11-14; 1 Peter 1:17-21; Revelation 5:9-10
	Freedom	He has set you free from anything that binds you.	You feel boxed in, stifled, trapped.	Luke 13:10-17; John 8:30-36; Romans 6:6-23; Galatians 5:1; Hebrews 2:14-15

APPENDIX 2

On Art Lessons

The gallery of gospel images we have from the Bible evangelists is our community's definitive collection. They are our touchstone, what we judge our words by, where we go back to learn. But we too are evangelists, painting pictures of Christ and his work for the world. The purpose of this book is not only for you to take the beauty here into your own life, but also for you to better show it to others. So here I suggest exercises in telling the gospel.

I'm going to ask you to take one image at a time and work on using it to portray the gospel. Art lessons, or any lessons really, are focused exercises to gain skill. One day you work on shapes, another on light and shading, another on blending colors. So I will guide you into using each of these images, in turn, to convey the gospel to a friend. Now, in this book I make a big point of how we need multiple images from the gallery to adequately preach the gospel. But one can't learn everything at once. Picking up one tool or technique at a time and working awhile with it is the best way to learn both what it can and what it can't do.

Of course, you will want to work with the lesson on your own for a while, but then you should go show someone. There needn't be any performance pressure; just ask a friend, "Do you mind if I run something by you? You know I am serious about Jesus, and I have been trying to figure out how to understand and talk about him better. Could I show you what I'm learning and have you tell me what you think?" No tricks. You're just asking a friend for feedback and help. (If they ask, "Are you saying I need to hear about Jesus?" Well, you'll have to answer honestly.

But it could be a good conversation to have.) I'm not writing a script for your life here; I want to put tools into your hands. So I will set out lessons and hope that they will be some help to you.

THE EXERCISES

First, you'll want to *review* the image. Look back over the chapter, see the chart in appendix one, and look up the passages in the chart and perhaps in the chapter.

Then you'll want to *compose* your telling of the gospel. Shoot for some notes that would prompt you to explain it verbally in one to three minutes, or you might just want to write it out in about two to three paragraphs. I am suggesting that you structure your story around the following plot:

Where we were (what we are saved *from*)

What God did (in Jesus)

Where God brings us (what we are saved *for*)

How we respond (how the images speak "repent and believe")

Another idea would be to center your gospel telling not around an outline, but around one of the passages given. This might not hit every point in the outline, but it would be more concrete and perhaps much easier to remember. With a summary, portability matters.

Remember to *illustrate* the power of the gospel from your life or the story of someone you know.

When you have finished, *ask* yourself where this telling felt strong and where it felt weak. For whom in your world would it be good news?

So go ahead and practice. If practice won't make you perfect, at least it can make you familiar, and that will go a long way toward making you ready to share the good news.

A SAMPLE "ART LESSON": LIFE

To speak the gospel with any of these images, we need to use them to interpret the life, death and resurrection of Jesus. Then we use their terms to call people to a response to Jesus, showing them the blessings he offers for this life and the life to come.

So, use the terms, Scriptures and ideas from this image to talk about . . .

What we've been saved *from:*

- *In the present:* There is a creeping death in our bodies, our spirits and our society that we cannot escape.
- *In the future:* Separated from the life of God, we can look forward only to the death of our bodies and our spirits.

What God has done in Jesus:

- As Jesus lived, he revealed the life of God to us.
- At the cross he was giving up his life for us, so that we might take up his.
- The resurrection was a victory for life; his kind of life not only survives death but also defeats it.

What we've been saved *for:*

- *In the present:* Jesus can take our sufferings and limitations and turn them into places of life, joy and freedom.
- *For the future:* Even the wonderful blessings of the present are only a foretaste of the life to come. We are promised a share in the resurrection life of Jesus.

How we respond to him:

- *Repent:* We must stop trying to grab life in our own power, stop pursuing our schemes for building a life for ourselves.
- *Believe:* We must accept the life he is calling us to in Jesus.

It might be simplest, especially at first, to wrap this gospel telling around one passage or story that centers on this image. You could experiment with one of the passages below. Feel free to paraphrase.

- Mark 8:27—9:1 (Jesus calls his disciples to lose their lives in order to save them.)
- John 11:1-44 (The story of Jesus, the resurrection and the life, raising Lazarus from the dead.)
- Romans 5:12—6:14 (Paul talks about dying and rising with Christ.)

APPENDIX 3

A Portable Gallery, or "How Can I Remember Twenty-Nine Gospels?"

While we want to have experienced and to know the language of many gospel images, we can only have so much at our fingertips, especially at first. So here is an idea for choosing some tellings of the gospel to have most ready.

I suggest that you have three of the images ready-to-hand. You should choose one from each of the three sections: images of life, images of mercy and restoration, and images of deliverance. So you might pick, for example, life and forgiveness and salvation. Or adoption and justification and freedom.

Having one from each of the three major groups will give you a healthy variety to offer. Left to ourselves, we might follow our own temperament or the leanings of our church tradition and choose all one type of image. This spread will help safeguard against imbalances and give you images that will fill in each other's weak sides.

But when choosing which of the three *within* a section to pick, I advise you to choose what you like best. Choosing your favorite, what resonates with you, is a way of following your intuition. You probably have a good feel for what will help you connect with your context and speak out of your own life with power. Go with it.

So pick these three and think through them. Pray through them (perhaps with the exercises in the next appendix). Practice speaking them. Let them be a place to start the good news getting into you more—and out from you more.

Appendix 4

Praying Through the Images

This appendix offers three reflection exercises. The first two meditations are for getting the gospel into you. Meditation one is more "defensive" or problem-oriented; with it you will use the different images to work through one particular concern in your life. Meditation two is more "offensive" or growth-oriented; with it you'll be looking to grow in your ability to see your whole life through some aspect of the gospel. Meditation three is direct preparation for getting the gospel out, thinking how it will connect with people in your life.

In the instructions below, when I say to think over, pray through or meditate on, do what works for you. If sitting down in a quiet place and closing your eyes makes you sleepy, get active. Write down your thoughts, questions and responses. Walk around and talk out loud. (If you are in public, just talk into your cell phone—no one will think twice.) And no one is saying you have to pray alone; get a friend to pray with you. Or get together with your Christian group and think these things through as a community. Just find some time and space that works for you and go there regularly. If these exercises help you there, good. If not, God will have some other good gift for you. Just go and talk with him.

Meditation 1

Here you can pray through an area or concern in light of the power of the gospel. The idea is to pick a problem or area of your life and bring it under the lens of each image in turn.

For example, let's say I have a problem with fear and anxiety. I would sit down and begin to ask, What does it mean to me here that God has given me an indestructible new *life*? How would believing it change how I think and act in this area? Then, after I had thought through the gospel image of life, I would move on. Okay, now what does it mean here that I am a *child* of God? How does this answer my fears? I would think through what this image tells me until I was ready to move on to the next. Now, I am a member of a *kingdom* that cannot be shaken, so now how should I feel, and so on.

Now your turn. Choose a situation or area of your life that you'd like help on. It could be a sin you are trying to overcome, a relationship you'd like to see go better, a decision you are trying to make or just some situation you are trying to cope with.

For starters, let me suggest you take ten to fifteen minutes on each image. (This may mean that you can't do all nine in one sitting. That's fine. Just do what you have time for and come back later.)

Begin with the chart in appendix one. Refresh your mind on that image. Read the verses given there, and begin to pray through the following questions:

- What light does this image shed on my situation?
- How does it show me what Jesus does for me?
- What hope does it offer me?
- As I step back and see this picture, what language do I have now for praising and thanking God?

When you are ready, move on to the next image.

A few notes about this, or any exercise: Expect it to feel a little forced and foreign at first. It's a new structure and it will likely feel stiff. Some parts of it will work for you better than others. Just see it through for a few rounds. Keep your expectations a little light at first. In time, you'll make the routine more your own and learn how to make it work for you. What we are after here is a habit of mind that turns to the gospel for light and hope. Be patient and seed the actions that will grow that habit.

MEDITATION 2

This is an exercise in "soaking in" a gospel image. Here, instead of picking a problem and bringing every gospel image to bear on it, the idea is to start with an image of the gospel and to drag every area of your life under its light.

For example, this week it could be time to practice thinking through *adoption*. So you dwell on it in prayer in the morning, and through the day you remember it. Fixing breakfast for the family, you might think, *I am one of God's children, and these kids here and I all have the same good Father.* Or walking down the street or across campus, *How does the Father feel, watching all these children of his run around all day and hardly ever think of him?* When you go to bed, you could picture the Father laying you down to rest and guarding you while you sleep After a week, you could be well on your way to having a well-fitting pair of gospel "glasses" for looking at life.

Here's how you might work this reflection and prayer into your week:

Sunday evening, take some time to load the image into your mind. Read through all the passages on that image from appendix one. Read through the chapter in this book if it helped you. That's it, no deep study, just a look before you plunge in. As you go to bed, ask God to help you wake up ready to see more of him.

Monday through Friday, follow a pattern like this:

In the morning, spend some time bringing the truth of this image to mind. There are five passages for each image on that summary chart, one for each day. They could work well done in order. Take one of the passages and study it. Consider these questions:

- How is the author using the image in this context? What picture is he trying to paint for you?
- How might this truth about the gospel change the way you think about the world? What does it say about people, about our society, about you?
- How is that image supposed to move or encourage you?

Now, look forward to your day:

- Can you see that Jesus is there, in the various places you'll be today?
- What does he have to offer you as you go through your day?
- How does he see the people you are rubbing shoulders with?
- What might he call you to do?

Ask him for eyes to see him and ears to hear him as you go out into your day.

During the day, the idea will be to remember this new way of seeing things, to let the gospel truth shape how you think about your day. I suggest you take along some concrete reminder of the truth you are trying to remember. I tend to like a business card with a verse written on it. As my hand slips into my pocket throughout the day, the verse comes to mind and I look up, remembering that this truth is about the situation I am in at the moment. You may choose some other small token. You might find it useful to have a different one for each image you are practicing.

This may feel a little like voodoo to you if you are not used to it. But really, we are just using props to train our minds. We respond to what is in our world. For instance, magazines and advertisements are scattered along my path, so it's no surprise I often think of yesterday's news or tomorrow's purchase. This physical reminder is just something we cast ahead into our day so that we can remember something worth thinking about.

As you remember, have a few simple questions you always ask:

- What does it mean that my Father (or Savior, or King) is here?
- How does he think about these people?
- How can I act as if this were true?

In the evening, take a few minutes before sleep to recall what you saw during the day, what you heard from the Lord. Try out your gospel vocabulary in thanking and praising him.

Saturday, let me suggest that you find a friend and tell him or her, over a nice cup of something, what you learned over the week. Also feel free to share some questions. Often when we begin to really look and think, we find more questions than answers. Both can lead us on to Jesus.

Sunday, you should take a break, of course.

MEDITATION 3

Here is a chance to focus outward with the gospel truth. This exercise will have you looking at a person or group and asking how the gospel is good news to them.

First, *pick a person or group* of people. They could be your parents, your children, the people in your dorm, your employees, people who are annoying you or people you'd like to know better. The question now is, How is the gospel good news to them?

Then *recall a gospel image* to mind, using the verses you can find in appendix one or others you have found along the way.

- Then *come into the presence* of the Lord and talk with him about them:

- This image deals with some problem in themselves or in their world. *Does this match up with anything I have heard them mention or complain about? Does it match up with needs I see in them?*

- This image speaks of good things that Jesus can bring his people. *Does this match up with any hopes or dreams I've heard from them? Does it speak to things I have often wished they had?*

- This image shows how Jesus can act powerfully in their lives. *What do they need Jesus to do for them?*

Talk this out with God, write it down in a journal, or pray it through with a friend. When you have done this with one image, pick up another. Remember to do more than just think about these people; talk to God about them. Ask him how he sees them, and leave some space in case he wants to answer and bring things to your mind. Ask him for in-

sight and, finally, if you can, have an active role in bringing the good
news to them.

As you go through this exercise, you may well find that you don't
know these people as well as you thought. That's fine. All sorts of things
come to light when we actually start thinking and praying over our lives.
It's better to be aware of ignorance than to be ignorant of it. And these
very questions you are asking God can lead you to be a better friend.
With questions in your mind, you will be more observant and hopefully
even more concerned. Just keep watching and praying, "Ask, seek,
knock . . . the door will be opened."

If you do feel you have come to some clarity on how to pray for these
people, be bold and persistent. God has always wanted to give these people what you are now asking. He will find a way to honor your prayers,
small and limited as they are. He will be delighted that you are now join-
ing him in caring for people he loves.

And be brave enough to offer yourself as part of the solution for these
people. Your part may go beyond prayer, or it may not. Just be careful to
obey what he tells you, because that is your own path deeper into the
gospel. Someone out there is probably praying for *you*, that you yourself
will get just that chance to know God better—and that you will take it.

NOTES

Chapter 1: Enter the Gallery
[1]John Stott, *The Cross of Christ* (Downers Grove, Ill.: InterVarsity, 1986), p. 168.
[2]*The Book of Common Prayer*, rev. ed. (New York: Seabury, 1953), p. 81.
[3]Leon Morris, *The Atonement* (Downers Grove, Ill.: InterVarsity Press, 1983), p. 203.
[4]Athanasius "On the Incarnation," in *Christology of the Later Fathers,* ed. Edward Hardy (Philadelphia: Westminster Press, 1954), p. 74.
[5]Ibid., p.108.
[6]Joseph A. Harriss, photographs by Eric Sander, "Master Class," *Smithsonian*, October 2002 <smithsonianmagazine.com/issues/2002/october/master.php>.

Chapter 2: Life: Born from Above
[1]Thomas à Kempis *The Imitation of Christ*, trans. Justin McCann (New York: Mentor-Omega, 1957), p. 37. À Kempis is here quoting Seneca.
[2]J. R. R. Tolkien, *The Return of the King* (Boston: Houghton Mifflin, 1965), p. 309.
[3]C. S. Lewis, *Mere Christianity* (New York: MacMillian, 1952), pp. 59-60.

Chapter 3: Adoption: Chosen in Love
[1]George MacDonald, *Unspoken Sermons* (Whitehorn, Calif.: Johannesen, 1997), p. 276. *Unspoken Sermons* was originally published in three parts, in 1867, 1885 and 1889.
[2]Ibid., pp. 284-85.
[3]C. S. Lewis, *Mere Christianity* (New York: MacMillian, 1952), pp. 59-60.

Chapter 4: Kingdom: A Good World Order
[1]Jesus' clearing of the temple is told in all four gospels: Mark 11; Matthew 21; Luke 19 and John 2.
[2]"Scottish Explorer David Livingstone," accessed August 15, 2006, at <www.scotlandvacations.com/livingstone.htm>.

[3]Tertullian *Apology* chap. 39, accessed August 15, 2006 at <www.ccel.org/ccel/schaff/
anf03.iv.iii.xxxix.html>.

[4]A good, concise biography of Wilberforce is the Trinity Forum Reading by John Pol-
lock, *William Wilberforce: A Man Who Changed His Times* (McLean, Va.: Trinity Forum, 1996).

[5]See Don Richardson, *Eternity in their Hearts* (Ventura, Calif.: Regal, 1984).

[6]The book Maria read was Gary Haugen's *Good News About Injustice* (Downers Grove,
Ill.: InterVarsity Press, 1999).

Introduction to Part 2

[1]*The Book of Common Prayer*, rev. ed. (New York: Seabury, 1953), p. 6.

Chapter 5: Justification: Being Right with God

[1]A number of people have helped me over the years to understand the Old Testament
grounding of this image. Most recently, I have found N. T. Wright's work very helpful, and it informs much of how I picture the court here. See *What Saint Paul Really
Said* (Grand Rapids: Eerdmans, 1997), pp. 29-37.

[2]Charles Wesley, "And Can it Be."

[3]Wright, *What Saint Paul Really Said*, p. 159.

Chapter 6: Forgiveness: Picking Up the Bill

[1]John Calvin, *Institutes of the Christian Religion*, vol. 20 of Great Books of the Western
World, trans. Henry Beveridge (Chicago: Encyclopædia Britannica, 1990), p. 290.

[2]Ibid., p. 281.

Chapter 7: Atonement: Taking Away Our Shame

[1]You can find one very helpful overview of how the gospel answers shame and guilt
in Norman Kraus, *Jesus Christ Our Lord* (Scottdale, Penn.: Herald Press, 1990), pp.
205-17.

[2]Thomas Oden, *The Word of Life* (San Francisco: Harper Collins, 1989), p. 368.

[3]I need to admit that Paul says this in the midst of using the justification image and
not the atonement image. However, there are several reasons I think it fits in this
discussion. First, all the images hang on our union with Christ in his death and resurrection—and this is a beautiful and clear statement of that union that could serve
any of the gospel images. Second, the crucifixion by its nature was truly meant to
bring shame on the victim and his people, to state what a failure they were and the
fate awaiting all such. Because of these two things and the simple and vivid nature
of this picture, it can be a center for our thinking about his bearing not only the penalty of our sins but their shame as well.

Chapter 8: Salvation: The Mighty Hand of God

[1]Bernard of Clairvaux, *The Nativity*, trans. Leo Hickey (Dublin: Scepter Ltd., 1959), p. 66.
[2]Ibid.
[3]Ibid.
[4]Ibid.
[5]George MacDonald, *Unspoken Sermons* (Whitehorn, Calif.: Johannesen, 1997), p. 291. *Unspoken Sermons* was originally published in three parts, in 1867, 1885 and 1889.

Chapter 9: Ransom and Redemption: Love Pays

[1]Leon Morris, *The Atonement* (Downers Grove, Ill.: InterVarsity, 1983), p. 107.
[2]What might it have cost God to send the plagues on Egypt? Well, if he was some distant Olympian deity, who didn't mind tossing down a few thunderbolts now and then, it wouldn't have cost him much. But if this was indeed the same God whom the Israelites were to come to know, then "The LORD is good to all; / he has compassion on all he has made" (Psalm 145:9). He cares for all his creation, even when he has to send disaster for his greater purposes. If this is the God and Father of our Lord Jesus Christ, then he is close to the hurting, even when he must judge and discipline. He was with every Egyptian in their pain and sorrow, and even in their dying. We must always see God through the lens of Jesus. Then we can read Exodus and see what most of the Israelites were not yet ready to see: a God who loved and grieved over the Egyptians, and was bleeding and dying for them even as he judged their sin. God values all the people he has made and has paid dearly for them.

Chapter 10: Freedom: Free for Life

[1]The United Nations Children's Fund (UNICEF), *The State of the World's Children 2006* (New York: UNICEF, 2005), pp. 50-51.
[2]Amy Wallace, "Jamie Lee Curtis: True Thighs," *More*, September 2002 <more.com/more/story.jsp?storyid=/templatedata/lhj/story/data/jamieleecurtistruethighs_08212002.xml>.
[3]Charles Wesley, "And Can It Be."

ABOUT THE AUTHOR

Neil Livingstone has served on the staff of InterVarsity Christian Fellowship for over twenty years, watching the gospel take root in the lives of college students and the leaders who serve them. Along the way he's picked up a master of arts in theology from Fuller Theological Seminary, and a passion to see the deep resources of the Scripture help Christians speak to today's world. Currently, Neil serves on InterVarsity staff in the metro D.C. area with his wife, Renea, and together they are raising three teenage daughters.

If you would like to contact Neil about speaking to your group or just to dialogue, or if you would like more resources on images of the gospel, please visit www.picturingthegospel.com.